FAITH AND MORAL AUTHORITY

Faith and Moral Authority

by

BEN KIMPEL

Professor of Philosophy, Drew University

PHILOSOPHICAL LIBRARY
NEW YORK

To my mother and father

CONTENTS

CONTENTS

well-being.

Such directives, for example, constitute the mores of a particular culture; the accepted standards of behavior in a community; the sanctioned codes for living as recommended in a

Preface

The purpose in writing this essay is to point out some of the
problems with which a reflective individual is confronted in
his attempt to understand the significance of moral principles.
It is acknowledged at every turn that such an inquiry encoun-
ters many perplexing difficulties. But to acknowledge that
there are difficulties in interpreting the function of principles
in human life is one thing: to maintain, however, that principles are morally irrelevant is quite another thing.

A belief which is basic to this essay is that an individual
cannot even evaluate particular choices or actions without
employing some standard. Any standard, however, by which
such an evaluation is made is a moral principle. It is a moral
principle, inadequate though it may often be, just because
it is used as a criterion for passing judgment upon the suitability of choices or actions in terms of their significance for
life.

A moral principle, therefore, is not experience. It is rather
a pattern according to which an individual may make choices
and so select experiences. Although the value of a principle
as a moral directive becomes apparent to an individual only
in experience, it does not follow that it is therefore only a
feature of experience. The moral value of a principle, it is
maintained in this essay, is its adequacy for directing individuals to make choices which contribute either to their own
well-being or to the well-being of others. The effectiveness
of a moral principle is its suitability as a directive in the en-

1

richment and ennoblement of human life, which is moral well-being.

In all corporate human life certain principles are respected as directives which stipulate an individual's responsibilities. Such directives, for example, constitute the *mores* of a particular culture; *the accepted patterns* of behavior in a community; the *endorsed codes* for living as recommended in a religious institution; *the commandments* as stated in a religious scripture. One fundamental moral problem is to evaluate the suitability of such directives. Yet, in evaluating them, an individual ought to acknowledge that although some time-honored principles are morally deficient, his understanding of the moral value of other principles may be less than it might be. In the first case, his moral responsibility is to reject the principles as unworthy to influence his decisions. But in the other case, his responsibility is to do what he can to understand more completely the principles, to the end that he may attain all the directive benefit he can from them in making his decisions. A failure, however, to conform to the directions of a principle is a commentary not upon the principle as a pattern of possible acting, but upon the use of the principle.

An earnest desire to acquire instructive directions how to live well motivates a sustained reflection on moral problems. But there may be reflection on moral problems without a faith that there are trustworthy principles by which such problems may be clarified. There are, in fact, modern philosophies which discredit the belief that there are principles which are dependable directives for human life. Acknowledging this fact, Pope Pius XII recently declared that " a new conception of moral life" is becoming more and more widespread, and it is stated in one form or another in various modern philosophies. Common to these philosophies is a confident dogmatism that no *general* principles can be known

2

for the dependable direction of human life. This point of view, although often stated in academic philosophies, is far from being merely an academic matter. It cuts at the very foundation of religious faith that there are principles, such as the Ten Commandments or the Beatitudes, which are trustworthy directives for all human life. The several philosophies which Pope Pius XII enumerates as examples of this point of view are "ethical existentialism, ethical actualism, ethical individualism." To this list, however, one may well add other contemporary philosophies, such as pragmatisms, radical empiricisms, behaviorisms, relativisms, and subjectivisms.

Common to all of these positions is a predominant emphasis upon *the individual's experience* as the sole possible content of his knowledge. When interpreted as moral philosophies, these popular theories maintain that an individual alone is aware of *his own* requirements; and so likewise, he alone is able to know the means which are most effective for fulfilling his requirements. These philosophies, therefore, are not only explicitly anti-authoritarian: they are also implicitly anarchistic. Such an anarchistic implication is as obvious in some of these modern philosophies as it is in the philosophies of the Greek Sophists. These philosophies emphasize the particular individual; *his* experiences; *his* requirements; *his* freedom, to the complete exclusion of all institutionally endorsed directives which might function as helpful instructions in making his decisions. A notion, therefore, which is common to these philosophies is that the only opportunity for an individual to be creative, and so to be "morally free," is to live without benefit of *general* principles, since principles as general directives are not unique.

The point of view basic to this essay, on the other hand, is that an individual cannot achieve a morally ordered life without some directives which have been learned from others, any more than he can achieve a significant science if he were to dispense with all instruction from others. To attempt to order one's life without the benefit of some principles learned from an institutional tradition is about as sensible as it is to attempt to develop one's own science without the benefit of some instruction from others. This point of view does not minimize the significance of the individual, for it ought to be perfectly clear that no directives, whether they are scriptural or conventional, are substitutes for an individual's responsibility to interpret them and to apply them in the particular situations in which he makes his own decisions. Yet, some modern philosophies which stress the *unique* nature of the individual ignore the very function of institutions in the creation of the content of an individual's life. To ignore such institutions from which an individual learns the minimum rudiments of his morality is, however, to ignore one of the fundamental points in a sound moral philosophy.

It is almost too obvious to mention that each individual must make his own decisions, in so far as such decisions are an individual's opportunity. But in doing so, an individual may well have the benefit of an institution which preserves directives that are capable of contributing effective help to him in the specific situations in which he must make his decisions. Thus one responsibility with which a morally serious individual is confronted is to understand as completely as he can the instructive function of principles which are *worthy to be respected* as directives in his life.

Yet, an unwillingness to admit the soundness of this point of view is a characteristic feature of our age. The popularity of existentialism; of philosophies of existence; of pragmatisms; of subjectivisms of every conceivable variety, reveals an attempt to find enlightenment in an individual's own life without benefit of instruction from an institution. A significant factor, however, which must be taken into account in diagnosing the widespread disorder in modern life is the attempt to create a corporate order with individuals whose lives are not ordered by principles suitable to be directives in human relations. An attempt, therefore, to understand the moral necessity for principles as directives in human life underlies the interpretation in this essay of moral responsibility and moral authority. That there are principles which may be known as helpful directives, and which may become the effective authority by which an individual orders his life to the moral end of living well, is the type of faith which is interpreted in this study.

I should like to acknowledge my gratitude to my assistant, Marjorie B. Chambers, for her kindness in reading the proofs.

B.K.

Drew University,
Madison, New Jersey.

Chapter One

THE NATURE OF MORAL PHILOSOPHY

1. *Defining the term moral*

The term *moral* sooner or later comes up in many discussions. Many individuals use the term, but it is not likely that everyone is aware of just what he means by the term. The very question, however, "What is the meaning of the term *moral*?", is itself the beginning of a reflection common to moral philosophies. A moral philosophy is an expression of interest in the sense of the term *moral*.

The term *moral* is derived from the Latin *mos, moris,* which is ordinarily translated *custom*. It is this sense of the term *moral* which accounts for the term *mores* as used in sociologies. Although this term is commonly used in social studies, the sense of the term is not always clear. It is used with various senses. A standard definition of the term, however, may be found in a dictionary which defines *mores* as "fixed customs imbued with an ethical significance." But just what "ethical significance" means is the very problem of what *moral* means. Little help is found in tracing the derivation of *ethical* from the Greek *ëthos,* since this term is commonly translated "custom."

What one learns from a dictionary is primarily a derivation of the term *moral*. Valuable as this information may be, it certainly is not the solution of a perplexing problem. One

who looks in a dictionary for a definition of the term *moral,*
and finds it given in terms of *custom,* is confronted with a
problem. It is the problem why there should be so much concern with the moral significance of behavior if the sense
of moral is synonymous with custom. The very doubt that
they are synonymous, however, is itself an expression of some
progress in an analysis of the nature of morality.

If the term *moral* were satisfactorily defined in terms of
custom, no one would spend much time reflecting on the
nature of morality. One would merely observe the patterns
of life which have been *endorsed* or *accepted* in a society. After
observing the patterns which have been accepted in a society,
he would then find out what *moral* means in that society.
Moral would then be a feature which all accepted patterns of
activity share in common by virtue of the fact that they are
accepted in a group and thus are given the status of social
acceptability.

2. *Searching for a moral criterion*

If after observing behaviors which are accepted in a community, one should wonder what justifies their acceptance,
he would have begun to reflect upon the problem of a moral
criterion. One questions the *moral* value of some behavior in
distinction to the moral value of other behavior only when he
employs some standard or criterion of what is *worthy of acceptance.* This very distinction between patterns of conventionally approved behavior which are worthy of acceptance
and those which are not is a moral scrutiny of customs. Such
scrutiny, however, would never occur if everyone were satisfied
to accept as satisfactory what has been endorsed by some
communities as the standard of morality itself.

An individual rebels against some customs, such as a
former Chinese practice of binding the feet of babies, or
against a former Hindu custom of cremating a wife on the

funeral pile of her husband. Passing judgment upon customs, approving some, and censoring others, is, however, not itself moral philosophizing. It is only an expression of one activity which could give rise to a moral philosophy, provided an individual were to reflect upon the standard he uses in making his judgment. When one becomes aware of the standard he uses as the norm by which he selects and rejects customs for their effect upon human life, he philosophizes. His philosophizing is a reflective examination of the significance of patterns of behavior in terms of life. This interest to consider the *life-significance* of a pattern of behavior is the underlying motive of an individual who spends time to think on the problem of life as it is affected by the patterns of behavior according to which individuals, and groups of individuals, live. The interest in this problem is not satisfied simply by possessing historical information of social practices, customs, mores, or whatever other term one may use to designate patterns of behavior which are *accepted* or *endorsed* by a group, or a community.

A moral philosophy begins to emerge as the result of an individual's reflection upon customs from the point of view of their justification, or warrant, as standards to which an individual is required to conform. This is at least one problem with which an individual may struggle when he begins to think about the problem of selecting from among possible patterns of life the patterns which have the greatest likelihood of constituting a helpful guide in living. The very desire to find a guide in life which is worth the effort to search for it is one motive which underlies an earnest and sustained reflecting, out of which have developed the diverse systems of moral philosophy.

The interest of an individual to find some standard, or norm, by which he may distinguish what is worthy of acceptance from what is not worthy of acceptance—even though a community or an entire nation might regard it as acceptable—underlies a moral philosophy as a *normative* study. Sociology, or specifically anthropology, is not a normative study. It could not be if it were to be "scientific." As "scientific," its obligation is to observe and to record characteristic features discernible in the behavior-patterns of a community. The fulfillment of this responsibility is, however, not enough to satisfy the individual who is interested in passing judgment upon the *warrant,* or the *justification,* for a person, or a people, to conform to some practices. The very fact that the Chinese practice of foot-binding and the Hindu practice of suttee are now obsolete is a concrete expression of the effect of moral judgment upon practice.

Before anyone, however, can be consistent in his evaluations of social practices, so that he rejects and selects with a thoughtful plan, he must have some standard by which he estimates what is worth conforming to, and what is not worth conforming to. The principle by which he passes such judgments, and makes such selections and rejections, is a moral norm. A *moral norm* is a principle which one regards as a standard worthy enough to be used in passing judgment upon particular practices. Thus, before a practice, or a pattern of life, can be evaluated for its worth in terms of life, one must have a standard. The standard by which he makes such an evaluation is a moral norm. A moral norm, therefore, is a principle which one accepts as a warranted criterion for passing judgment upon patterns of behavior. Hence, the formulation of a moral norm is not only a product of a classroom exercise. It is also the implied objective of everyone who earnestly thinks about the life-significance of activities or patterns of behavior.

The formulation of a norm by which one may evaluate the worth of a pattern of life is not the result of so-called "abstract" thinking; and it is not the product of what some

9

like to disparage as "detached" reflection. It is rather the outcome of observing what has been practiced by people, and then observing the effects which such practices have had upon the quality of their lives. Such a correlation of the pattern of behavior and the consequences of the pattern in terms of the quality of life makes the difference between a scientific study of human life, such as sociology, and a philosophical study of life, such as moral philosophy. The difference is not in the material studied. It is a difference in the method. One method is an accurate *enumeration* of what is observed. The other is an *evaluation* of what is observed. It is a judgment upon the worth of practices in terms of their influence upon the quality of life. When conformity to a group-endorsed pattern is regarded as a contribution to the enrichment of well-being in human life, it is looked upon as morally worthy. Such conformity is morally worthy in the sense that it is worth practicing; and the pattern of behavior to which one conforms is regarded as justifying such conformity.

Any such selection, or rejection, from among the multiplicity of practices in community life is, however, the expression of a consistent application of a principle only when an individual has clearly defined a *standard of moral worth*. The sustained and earnest effort to reflect upon human practices to the end that one may arrive at a principle for interpreting the worth of practices in terms of their contribution to life is moral reflection; and such reflection may be carried on in classrooms, as well as outside classrooms. Anyone who is capable of sustained and consistent thinking qualifies for this undertaking.

The more one knows about the actual practices of men, the more material he has with which to reflect. "The fact is the starting-point," says Aristotle, and therefore, "we must begin with things known to us."[1] But the amount of such facts which constitute the informative equipment of an anthropologist is not the only condition for successful reflection on moral problems. What is essential for a moral philosophy is the capacity to see the relationship between *any* pattern of behavior and the consequences of the pattern in terms of the quality of life which is experienced by individuals when they conform to that pattern. This is not just an academic undertaking which is prompted by an intellectual curiosity to correlate data as if the qualitative differences in human life could be reduced to a study in keeping with Mill's Canon of Concomitant Variation. Any purely statistical interest in observing the effects which certain practices have in terms of the quality of human life is certainly not the motivating drive of moral philosophizing. The motive in an earnest reflection upon human life is the desire to interpret human life in order to discover principles for human life which are worth knowing.

A principle or pattern of life which is worth discovering to the end that it may be used as a guide, or a directive, is an *ideal*. It is an ideal in the sense that it is an idea which is worth accepting as a directive in life. Thus, any earnest reflection which endeavors to discover such ideals, or directives, which are worth conforming to in life is impelled by very practical motives. It is motivated by the desire to find what is worth knowing; and the most fruitful source for beginning such a search is the laboratory of human life itself. In this laboratory there is plenty of data to study, and there is sufficient material upon which one may well spend his time in careful thinking. But thinking about human behavior without a point of view to direct the thinking is not very productive. What makes the effort of reflecting upon human life contribute to a moral philosophy is the desire to discover a principle with which to evaluate the worth of practices. This interest in evaluating practices in terms of their significance for life is the practical motivation underlying a moral philosophy. Thus the interest which motivates such a study is not "scientifically" dispassionate. In so far as a moral philosophy arises out of the earnest search to find a principle which is worth becoming the directive of life, moral philosophizing is anything but dispassionate. It is passion for life, given direction by every accessible resource of intelligence.

3. *Searching for a practical principle for living*

The fact that morally motivated reflection is a search for a *principle* should not be construed to mean that it is a search for an abstraction from life. A principle which is applicable to all life would necessarily be more abstract than a principle applicable only to a very limited social context. If by "abstract" one means detached from *all* reference to practice, then no earnest moral philosophy ever has sought an abstract principle. If, however, by "abstract" one means a pattern which is general enough to be a standard or a directive for particular practices, then every moral philosophy seeks an "abstraction." The term "abstract," however, might well be avoided in a discussion of this type, since the very sense of what is "abstract," and what is not, has always been one of the controversial problems in the history of philosophy. It is, therefore, a matter of practical good sense not to increase the number of problems when one is trying to clarify a problem. It is enough to claim for moral philosophy that it is practical when it seeks to formulate a principle which may effectively be used in practice. "Will not the knowledge of it," Aristotle asks, "have a great influence on life? Shall we not, like archers who have a mark to aim at, be more likely to hit upon what is right?" [2]

Practice is always individual or particular. There is no such thing as "general practice." Every practice is a particular instance of behavior. But many instances of behavior may share a feature in common, and the observation that

12

there is a feature in common is abstracting. It is abstracting in the sense that it takes one feature shared in common by many instances and makes it a special object of attention. If such reflective activity in directed observing is abstracting, then every classification is an abstraction. A moral principle is likewise an abstraction in the sense that it is a feature which may be shared by particular patterns of behavior.

One objective of moral philosophy is to formulate such a principle which is inclusive enough to become the standard by which evaluations may be made when the significance for life is the problem which motivates reflection. The attempt to arrive at such a principle is the earnest undertaking of one who reflects on the problem of the sense of the term *moral*. What is *moral* then has features of a normative principle; and the principle is a moral norm in so far as it is a pattern of life which, when accepted as a guide in living, contributes to the enrichment of life. The effectiveness of a pattern of life for constituting a dependable directive in living, to the end of attaining an enrichment of life, is the moral value of a principle.

4. *Searching for a principle which is not limited to practice*

Anyone who is aware of the advantage of having a map by which he may find his way in a new territory also becomes aware that there would be equal advantage in having a rule by which he might be given suggestions for living. Just as a map is made by individuals who, by their own exploring, have found the lay of a land, so there are rules for living which have been formulated by individuals who have learned what might be helpful for others to know. The conviction that it is desirable to acquire whatever helpful guidance one can secure in living underlies all moral philosophy. Yet, anyone with intelligence enough to arrive at such a conviction will also very soon come to another conviction: he will be convinced that one cannot act upon every recommendation, just as one cannot follow every map. Some maps contradict other maps, just as some recommendations for living contradict other recommendations for living. When an individual is confronted by conflicting proposals, he becomes aware that, helpful though some recommendations may be, they also constitute a problem. It is the problem of evaluating them. The problem arises when an individual is aware of the need to select from among recommendations; and yet, such a selection cannot even be undertaken until he has some fairly clear idea of what type of suggestion to accept, and what type to reject. After one has reached this degree of understanding of the problem with which everyone is confronted who tries to think about the problem of finding his way most effectively in life, he has already started on the career of a moral philosopher.

An awareness that some recommendations for living contradict other recommendations is not only a birth of an awareness of the practical need to think consistently—which is a birth of respect for the principles of logic—but it is also a realization of the practical necessity to select from among such suggestions the ones which can fit into a consistent pattern for living. This awareness of the problem with which one is confronted when he is faced with mutually inconsistent proposals for living is the beginning of morally motivated reflection. Such morally motivated reflection is the first step in the formulation of a moral philosophy. This first step is stated by Plato as becoming aware of the fact that one cannot act consistently, any more than he can think consistently, when he does not have rules, or principles, for acting which are mutually consistent. One who tries to think, or to live, without some set of mutually consistent principles is, says Plato, like a man who "goes blinking about . . . first of one opinion then of another, and seems to have no intelligence." [3]

There is nothing strange about this. One cannot live with an order of intelligence in his life unless some intelligent direction is given to his life. The conviction that the attainment of a life of order is worth the effort to find a principle of order is the moral faith which underlies moral philosophy. A second conviction which underlies moral philosophy is also stated by Plato. It is that an individual's life "becomes orderly"[4] only when he conforms to an ordering pattern. The order in life which may be attained by conforming to a principle is the effect, and so the moral value, of a principle which stipulates the conditions for such an order. Hence, the discovery of a principle which is worth accepting as a guide in living is the most important single discovery which one can make in his life. One who does not believe this will never undertake to formulate a moral philosophy. But one who is convinced of this will at least, by virtue of his conviction, be prepared for the task. Plato, for one, was eminently prepared for this task on the basis of his conviction. He believed that unless we know a principle which is worth conforming to in our lives, all "other knowledge or possession of any kind will profit us nothing."[5] He likewise believed that such a principle can be effective in an individual's life only if he earnestly endeavors to interpret behavior in terms of a principle. Such a principle is not a particular behavior; and it is not a particular convention. Plato did not disbelieve in the moral value of all conventions; but when confronted by mutually inconsistent conventions, he believed that an individual is confronted with a profound moral problem. It is the problem of evaluating them in order to select from among them the ones which are compatible with the richest possible enlightenment of life. Plato was keenly aware of this problem, and so declared that "until the person is able to . . . define rationally the idea of good . . . he apprehends only a shadow."[6] He therefore was interested in finding a principle by means of which practices may be evaluated in order to ascertain their worth for life.

Thus one cannot understand Plato's moral philosophy with out also understanding that a basic motive in his reflecting is to discover a principle which is not itself a particular behavior, or a particular convention, but is a principle by which one may evaluate particular behaviors and particular conventions. The faith of Plato is that if one is to have the advantage of a directive for living which is both consistent and also *adequate,* he must go beyond particular practices to find, if possible, a principle. The faith that such a principle may be formulated which will function in life as a dependable directive is a Platonic conviction. All who believe this, think as Plato does in regards to one essential condition for moral philosophy. This faith is not a product of reflecting on the problem of life. It is a point of view; an attitude; or a conviction, with which one begins his reflecting.

A necessary condition for success in this reflective quest is, of course, intelligence enough to comprehend a principle. One cannot reflectively formulate a principle unless he can understand the nature of a principle. A principle is not a particular practice. It is a pattern of practice. Hence, only one who can understand the difference of particular practices and a principle of practice can make any progress in discovering a principle for evaluating practices. It is for this reason that Plato says that "philosophers only are able to grasp"[7] such principles. A philosopher, however, according to Plato is one who respects enlightenment sincerely enough to spend his life in an effort to become more enlightened than he would be if he did not spend such time. This qualification for a philosopher is not academic: it is a matter of faith.

Plato is a witness of the faith that a principle worth knowing can be known only by effort. Everyone who believes that there is a pattern for living which can be known, and can be known only by earnest searching, thinks as Plato does in this respect.

16

But such a search yields a moral philosophy about moral principles only when one has intelligence enough to understand principles. Principles are understood: conventional practices are observed. This distinction between the methods of reflectively knowing and empirically observing is fundamental to Plato's philosophy. Plato declares "the many (conventions) are seen but not known, and the ideas (principles) are known but not seen."[8]

This distinction between the methods for learning is basic to an understanding of Plato's philosophy, and yet, an unwillingness to admit the soundness of this distinction is a characteristic feature of our age. The widespread popularity of pragmatisms of every conceivable variety reveals how far many people today are from the point of view of Plato. The exaltation of practice is itself the principle by which many individuals attempt to live who justify their confusion on the grounds of confused philosophies. When Plato declares that the "uninformed of the truth . . . have no single aim of duty which is the rule of all their actions, private as well as public,"[9] he offers one diagnosis of what is wrong with individuals, caught in widespread disorder in living, and hence in profound dissatisfaction. A pragmatist does not believe that there are *supremely desirable* patterns for living, or *basic* moral principles. The only principles which can be known in practice are, according to pragmatists, products of practice. Thus the modern view of the pragmatists and the point of view of Plato could not be farther apart. The faith of Plato is that there is more to be known than practice, and even more than all patterns of conventionally accepted practice.

Plato is perfectly aware that his moral philosophy outlines a problem. He is entirely aware that he describes "a task which is really tremendous."[10] His moral philosophy is a statement of what would have to be done *if* an individual were to attain an enlightened life. Hence, no one can understand what Plato is speaking about without also understanding that he is not offering a rule of thumb by which one may live. There is no rule of thumb for living an enlightened life. Enlightened living is searching for enlightenment; and the search is directed with the faith that there are principles which *when known* will enlighten life. This is no contradiction. An individual searches because he is enlightened enough to believe that there is more to be known than is already known. The very search for such principles is, says Plato, directing one's mind toward that "which he sees neither injuring nor injured by one another."[11] Hence, the conviction that there is a reality worth knowing in life which is not a product of the struggle for survival, and it is not a pattern of the struggle, is itself a moral enlightenment. One who believes this is already enlightened enough to seek beyond the struggle for survival, and beyond conventions developed in the struggle, for more enlightenment than can be gained in such a struggle.

Men "live and grow"[12] in the search, and such a search is a directing of life. In the search, life becomes enlightened. The *enlightening* of life is an experience; the *enlightenment* of life is not an experience. The enlightenment of life is a feature of life. The faith of Plato is that there are principles other than human practice which can be known, and when known, human life will achieve a feature which is derived, not from the search, but in the search.

Plato refers to this principle as the "Idea of the Good," and interprets it as "the universal author of all things . . . right."[13] It is a feature common to all practices which are worthy of approval; but it is other than, and more than, the practices themselves. A comparable point of view is expressed in the religious faith which interprets the Ten Commandments as sharing in common the authority of God. Thus, the authority of God is more than the authority of each com-

18

mandment. All the Commandments share in the authority of God because such authority is more than each commandment. According to Plato, the Idea of the Good is the condition of all order, and hence, is the condition for the moral effectiveness of ordering principles in human life. This theory of reality thus underlies Plato's conviction of the possibility for discovering in life a universal principle for living. The Prologue to the Fourth Gospel likewise rests upon a comparable theory of reality. It is that there is a completely trustworthy reality that can be known which is dependable for all men, and hence is not a product of any social convention. It is uncreated; but awaits man's discovery. When men discover it, they become enlightened. Plato believes, as does the writer of the Fourth Gospel, that what men believe and do in no way constitutes the nature of all *possible patterns* of belief and practice. Possible patterns of acting, and possible patterns of belief, constitute a reality yet to be discovered. What men believe and do constitutes historical data: not the extent of reality; and not the scope of possible knowledge. The justification for human living, according to Plato, is to discover not only an ordering principle in life, but also to seek to know all one can of the principle of order. This principle of order Plato refers to as the Idea of the Good.

Professor Demos points out that for Plato "the Good is value in general, of which moral virtue is only a particular instance," and therefore "ethics . . . deals with specific values" which "need to be validated by a study of ultimate principles, and this is the study of the Good as such."[14] Plato believes that it is possible to have "a knowledge still higher than justice and other virtues" because he believes that there is a principle other than all particular moral values by which such particular values themselves may be evaluated. Yet, this is the very emphasis in Plato's philosophy which Aristotle criticized in formulating his own moral philosophy.

19

5. Stressing practice, and losing a principle for practice

Aristotle was not satisfied with the principle of moral value proposed by Plato. He maintained that if "the Idea of Good" is the principle of moral worth, then the basic criterion of morality is "empty."[15] He believed that it is "empty" in the sense that it does not state a rule for particular behaviors. Hence, he argued, it is not a moral standard according to which an individual may decide what ought to be done. It is rather a condition for the value of everything, and only incidentally has bearing upon human behavior.

Although Aristotle is quite justified in rejecting Plato's proposal of a principle on the grounds of its abstraction from practice, it is only fair to acknowledge that the objective of Plato is to formulate a principle that would *not* be limited to particular patterns of behavior. Thus, what Plato considers the function of a basic moral principle is not what Aristotle regards as the function of a moral principle. Plato believes that an analysis of moral values would be a consistent moral philosophy only if one were to have a principle which states the nature of all values. After knowing the nature of values, Plato assumes that one could then know what would be a particular value, and a particular behavior in human life would have particular moral value *if* it had features essential to all value. The very procedure of Plato in ascertaining the nature of value in order to formulate a principle of moral value is the fundamental point at which Aristotle differs from him.

Plato thinks as a logician: he is interested in classes, or types, and hence he interprets a moral principle as a type of structure common to morally valuable activities in human life. He believes that all discussions about morality could be given consistent direction only if one were to know the nature of value, or the nature of anything which is valued with real

20

warrant. Thus, he endeavors to formulate the most general principle of evaluation as the first condition for a moral philosophy. This obviously is taking the long way, and such a procedure is not congenial to anyone who is interested primarily in particular practices. Aristotle is interested in a practical scheme by means of which an individual may decide why one pattern of behavior is not worth desiring, and another is. One cannot, therefore, understand the moral philosophy of Aristotle unless he understands the practical concern of Aristotle. Aristotle believes that reflecting on morality is a practical necessity, in the sense of a necessity for practice. He even believes that this fact is so obvious that it is something to be taken for granted. Therefore he says, it is "a common principle and must be assumed": "we must act according to the right rule."[16] A knowledge of "a right rule" in behavior, is according to Aristotle, "practical wisdom."[17]

One can hardly overstress the fundamental difference in the emphases of Plato and Aristotle. Plato is convinced that an individual will understand why a particular behavior has moral value only when he knows what constitutes the nature of value. Aristotle, on the other hand, is equally convinced that some reflection has nothing whatsoever to do with practical problems. From his point of view, Plato's philosophy of value, and so Plato's moral philosophy, comes under the classification of reflection without practical bearing on life. Aristotle is convinced that a "rule," or principle, is a necessity for life, and hence its justification is practical. The very meaning of "virtue," he believes, depends not only upon acting "in accordance with the right rule," but also, knowing "the right rule."[18] This difference, according to Aristotle, makes the difference between morality and animal behavior. An animal might conform to a rule, just as well as an individual might. But Aristotle does not classify all behavior in conformity to a rule as "morally motivated." Only that behavior is morally motivated which conforms to a rule "present" in an individual as a guide which he himself *accepts* as his directive in life. According to Aristotle, "it is not merely the state in accordance with the right rule, but the state that implies the *presence* of the right rule, that is virtue."[19] Thus, a moral judgment is not passed upon animal activity for the reason that animals do not have the benefit of a principle, or "universal judgment," but act only on the basis of "memory of particulars."[20] Moral accountability in acting rests, according to Aristotle, on the fact that an individual can take into account in his acting more than an animal can take into account. This might be stated as a presupposition of moral responsibility: some individuals are able to take into account more factors in acting than any animal can. Animals may well remember consequences associated with particular patterns of behavior, and when so conditioned, avoid a particular activity. But the selective activity of an animal is not, according to Aristotle, the consequence of using a general rule of life. It is the result rather of a conditioning by particular conditions.

In his attempt, however, to formulate a principle for living, Aristotle became so concerned with practice that he lost sight of a basic moral criterion for evaluating practice. It may well be that Albert Schweitzer overstates the deficiency in Aristotle's philosophy when he says that Aristotle "brings together material for a monumental building, and runs up a wooden shack," but it is fair to point out, as Schweitzer does, that Aristotle "shirks the problem of the basic principle of the moral."[21] Yet, the criterion by which the philosophical value of a moral philosophy must be measured is the adequacy of a criterion in terms of which patterns of behavior are to be evaluated for their moral significance. Judged by this criterion, Aristotle is not successful as a moral philosopher. He does not formulate a basic principle which affirms why practices are morally valuable. He formulates, instead, only a formal criterion for selecting activities which are morally suitable. This criterion is the "mean between extremes." He says, "in all things the mean is praiseworthy, and the extremes neither praiseworthy nor right, but worthy of blame."[22] The mean is an intermediate; and consequently, "the intermediate state is *in all things* to be praised."[23]

According to this rule, there are only two features characteristic to all morally undesirable activities. They are "excess" and "deficiency."[24] An activity is morally praiseworthy when it is an intermediate between excess and deficiency. When an individual so controls his actions that his behavior is intermediate between excess and deficiency he fulfills his moral responsibility. Aristotle declares that "It is possible to fail in many ways (for evil belongs to the class of the unlimited, as the Pythagoreans conjectured, and good to that of the limited), while to succeed is possible only in one way."[25] The one fundamental moral obligation, therefore, is to "choose that which is intermediate, not the excess nor the defect."[26] Thus, according to this interpretation of morality as conformity to a mean between extremes, the basic moral responsibility is to ascertain what the mean is in activities in order to conform to the mean as ascertained.

One need not be a philosopher, however, to see that this is not a clarification of any problem in acting. It is rather a statement of a problem. The problem may be stated as a question: "What is the mean which is the condition for the moral value of an activity?" That this criterion does not clarify the problem of what is the mean for a particular individual is stated by Aristotle himself when he says that the "intermediate" is always "relative"[27] to the individual in a particular situation. One can readily see how little *practical* help an individual is afforded by this criterion when he follows Aristotle's analysis of particular moral virtues. For example: "The man, then, who faces the right things from the

23

right motive, in the right way and at the right time, and who feels confidence under the corresponding conditions, is brave."[28] And again: "The liberal man, like other virtuous men, will give . . . rightly; for he will give to the right people, the right amounts, and at the right time, with all the other qualifications that accompany right giving."[29] Justice is likewise defined in the same manner: "The just is the proportional; the unjust is what violates the proportion."[30] Thus, since "the middle state is praiseworthy," "we must cling to the middle state."[31]

One need not add more illustrative material to make the point that Aristotle has not clarified a single basic problem in his formulation of a practical rule for human life. On the basis of Aristotle's rule of the mean, there would be no sacrifice of life for a cause. There would not even be a devotion to a cause to the exclusion of every other interest in life, since wholehearted, single-minded devotion would be an excess. One does not need to study moral philosophy, nor does he need to have the reflective capacities of a philosopher, to see the full implications of Aristotle's doctrine of the mean as the norm of what is morally most to be respected. It is devoid of idealism, having even less idealism than much conventional morality. In conventional morality there are at least occasions when individuals become heroically sacrificial, and others have enough of the heroic in them to acknowledge such heroism. But the complete sacrifice of one's life is an act which cannot fit into the framework of Aristotle's moral philosophy. The product of Aristotle's reflecting without idealism is a moral philosophy without idealism.

The one morally most worthy undertaking in a reflectively directed life, according to Aristotle, is "to find the middle." But this undertaking is interpreted as an intellectual problem. Its success depends entirely upon knowledge. It depends upon knowing what is the mean in a particular act. The analogy which Aristotle offers of morally motivated reflection and a mathematician's calculation is instructive. It is instructive because it reveals how much idealism there is in the moral philosophy of Aristotle. According to Aristotle, "it is no easy task to find the middle." "To find the middle of a circle is not for everyone but for him who knows."[32]

But even if one were to admit that the intermediate, or mean, is a practical standard, he would still be confronted with the problem of deciding just which actions should conform to this rule of the intermediate. Aristotle himself declares that the rule does not apply to *all* actions. He says that "not every action nor every passion admits of a mean; for some have names that already imply badness, e.g. spite, shamelessness, envy, and in the case of actions, adultery, theft, murder; for all of these and such like things imply by their names that they are themselves bad, and not excesses or deficiencies of them."[33] Yet, one must wonder if Aristotle has done anything here except to list patterns of behavior which have already been classified by conventional morality as *vices*. The rule of the mean does not apply to behaviors which already are deficient or excessive. A fundamental question in a moral philosophy, however, is why some behaviors *should be* classified as vices. Aristotle does not raise this question, except to say that they are excesses. But many acts of self-sacrifice are also excesses. Hence the problem: "Just when is acting which is not a mean between extremes a vice; and just when is it not?" The answer to this question is not given by Aristotle; and it is not given because he does not examine *the basic principle* of moral values. He simply stipulates a formal rule by which one may classify particular behaviors as virtues, and others as vices. He endeavored to formulate a guide for practice without faith enough to refer beyond patterns of conventional practice; and consequently,

25

he did not formulate a criterion for evaluating the moral significance of conventional practice.

No one would deny that some knowledge is an essential condition for directing one's life in the achievement of what is consistently beneficial. But only one with the bias of philosophical rationalism would maintain the thesis that *the essential* condition for beneficial practice is a *strictly* intellectual accomplishment. Aristotle, however, makes it clear that reflection is not the sufficient condition for moral achievement when he says that "character must somehow be there already with a kinship to virtue, loving what is noble and hating what is base."[34] In this statement, therefore, he reveals an awareness of the profound *mystery* of moral faith itself. This mystery is the fact that one individual endeavors to use his intelligence for moral purposes, when another of equal, or even greater intelligence does not. Rationalistic moral philosophies are, consequently, superficial to the extent that they assume that a clarification of ideas is *the sufficient condition* for a moral use of resources for living.

Aristotle himself criticizes this extreme rationalism when he declares that "if without being ignorant a man does the things which will make him unjust, he will be unjust voluntarily."[35] Thus, even according to Aristotle, moral problems are more than intellectual matters; and an individual has more to do in a moral operation upon his life than to clarify his ideas.

Aristotle, for example, distinguishes between desire for what makes an individual self-indulgent, and a desire for self-indulgence. "No one craves to be self-indulgent," he says,[36] since self-indulgence is the result of inclinations asserting themselves without scrutiny of their morally adverse effects upon life. The significant point which Aristotle makes for a moral philosophy, however, is that the "incontinent man" does "things that he does not think he ought to do."[37] But it is just this contradiction between what an individual himself recognizes as an ought, or a responsibility, and what he actually does which brings an incontinent life into the category of moral responsibility. Incontinence would not even be a matter of an individual's moral responsibility if it were not within his control. An incontinence which an individual *cannot* control may be a matter for psychiatric help; but it would not be a matter of an individual's *own* responsibility.

One of the stern facts, however, which confronts an individual who reflects on the nature of morality is that an individual sometimes chooses what, in the very act of choosing, he himself recognizes as detrimental to himself, either directly or indirectly. Individuals, for example, who are aware that bribery in public office entails the impairment of the political structure of social life, and with its impairment the actual handicap to their own lives and the lives of all in whom they are concerned, nevertheless, accept bribes. Thus individuals, aware of the anti-social nature of their acts, do what is anti-social. This is a sobering fact; and discouraging as it may be, it nevertheless must be acknowledged in a moral philosophy. Yet, the notion that there is such an "irrationality" in a "reasonable" individual is a contradiction which rationalistic philosophies find intolerable. Hence, consistent rationalistic philosophies regard the contradiction as only an intellectual confusion, and consequently maintain that it can be removed exclusively by intellectual means. But the notion that this inconsistency is not a contradiction in the authorities by which an individual attempts to live means that an individual is not even prepared to take into account some of the most sobering data in human life.

Every sound moral theory must acknowledge this "irrationality." In acknowledging it, one comes to grips with the fact of the very difficulty of moral effort. Professor Royce puts his finger on this problem when he maintains that an individual "can through voluntary inattention freely choose to forget" what he has already acknowledged as an ought.[38] It is this narrowing of the field of attention which makes action less enlightened than an individual is reflectively aware it ought to be. It is this "irrationality" which Professor Bosanquet likewise has recognized when he points out that often "in willing . . . we know that we are willing against what is good."[39] Yet, willing against what is clearly recognized as having the right to command one's life constitutes a fundamental fact in the moral seriousness of human life. This deliberate disavowal of *a recognized ought* is not merely an intellectual disability. It is, as Professor Perry declares, a "moral failure."[40]

Although an individual may earnestly want to know the facts with which he ought to reckon in making a choice, he may nevertheless, err in judgment due to his deficient knowledge. Even when an individual does all that he can to avoid error in judgment, error is always a possibility, because the data taken into account are likely to be less than ought to be considered for his own well being, to say nothing about the well being of others. Theoretically, however, an individual who desires to know what he should take into account would be saved from error in actual judgment provided his zeal to acquire such knowledge were effectively to determine his actual knowing. But there is a type of error in judgment which extreme rationalism is not willing to acknowledge: it is an individual's *unwillingness* to face the "facts." Pride, for example, may blind an individual to the facts which contest his vanity; and so handicap him in gaining information even for his own advantage. Thus a vanity which moves an individual to refuse to acknowledge facts which are adverse to his own false estimate of himself is an "irrationality" in the very individual who is capable of reasoning. Although capable of reasoning from facts, an individual is also capable of misusing his capacity; thereby arriving at conclusions which

28

are false because the data upon which he reflects have been distorted. The very unwillingness, however, to acknowledge that what is uncomplimentary to a false pride too often is ignored prevents an individual from coping with the moral handicap itself of such a false estimate of himself.

This handicap is more fundamental than simply a deficiency in acquired information. It is an unwillingness to acquire information, because what *morally should be taken into account* runs counter to the false notion of what one actually is. For an individual who maintains such a false concept of himself, his intellectual capacity to consider data is biased by his unwillingness to face certain "facts."[41] Yet, an extreme rationalist does not admit that there is a *deliberate* refusal to take certain facts into account, which for *moral* purposes ought to be taken into account. The basic premise of a rationalistic moral philosophy is that man does *not willingly tolerate* an irrationality in his life. Irrationality, therefore, must be explained as a result of factors which are not essential to a "reasonable" individual.[42] But any such distortion of reflecting prevents an individual from coping with the fact of his own handicapped reflecting, since he is incapable of "reflecting" his own way out of distorted reflecting. His handicap is *his own* reflecting.

The type of reasoning which extreme rationalism cannot admit is a self-imposed deception. Yet, there is such deception imposed upon an individual by himself when his reflecting is biased by his own prejudices. The most difficult of moral achievements, in fact, rest upon the actual training of an ability to take into account *all* the data with which an individual *ought* to reckon, either for his own or for others' welfare. If an individual *cannot* take into account all the data which are relevant to an informed decision, he may not even be considered morally accountable for error in his judgment.

Reasoning is not dependable unless it is informed, and yet,

the very ease with which reasoning can arrive at false beliefs from inadequate data constitutes one of the most sobering facts in reflecting on the nature of moral responsibility.

The desire to know what one *ought to take into account* is a condition for achieving a knowledge which is morally adequate. An individual may well be mistaken in his belief of what is adequate; but mistaken as he may be, he will never make an effort to know more than he already assumes to know unless he is convinced that what he knows is morally insufficient. Yet, this is the very element of *faith* which is basic to all sustained effort to acquire knowledge for the purpose of enlightening life.

Chapter Two

MORAL PHILOSOPHY AND FAITH

1. The faith of Socrates

Different though the moral philosophies of Plato and Aristotle may be, they do, nevertheless, share in common the belief that reflective effort is justified by its beneficial contribution to human life. This conviction is a minimum condition for any moral philosophy. If an individual were not convinced that there is some justification for thinking about the problems of human life, he would not spend very much time reflecting in an attempt to formulate a moral philosophy. Plato and Aristotle, however, were convinced that reflection is morally justified. The basic conviction which continues from Socrates, through Plato, and into the life of Aristotle has well been called "the Great Tradition." It is "great" from the point of view of anyone who believes that only with earnest and consecrated reflection upon the problems of life can there enter into life a clarification of at least some problems. This continuity of conviction which links the three philosophers of ancient Greece into one tradition is the belief of every individual who undertakes a reflective examination of some of the perplexing problems in human life.

Socrates believed so strongly that a reflective examination of human life is essential to the very justification for living

31

that he declared, "The unexamined life is not worth living." Although convinced that reflection has preeminent significance in human life—even to the point of making the difference between finding a justification for living and not finding it—still, he did not formulate a thoroughly integrated moral philosophy. His most significant contribution to the history of moral philosophy is the affirmation of a faith which motivated his life-long reflective search. His life was a search for an understanding; and he never seriously doubted that understanding can be achieved for the enlightening of life.

He was convinced that no moral problem can be resolved merely by the method of consulting people to find out what they think. Interesting as it may be to know what people think, beliefs do not necessarily constitute a criterion with which to evaluate the moral significance of beliefs. The one conviction, therefore, which explains the earnest quest of Socrates is that "a question must be decided by knowledge, and not by numbers, if it is to have a right decision."[1] The qualification, "if it is to have a right decision," is the explanation why a knowledge of what others think is not all that is to be desired. No one becomes enlightened by knowing what others believe, unless what he believes is itself enlightened. But this is just the problem of a morally earnest life. It is to find out which beliefs are enlightened. When this is known, then an individual will know whom to believe.

The certification for the truth of beliefs, however, is not the fact that someone is convinced they are true. "The point is not who believes it," says Socrates, "but whether it is true," and by this he means that the criterion for the truth of belief is a feature of belief. A belief is true when the belief is informed. Thus a belief is true only when it has a specific property. Its informative value is the property which makes a belief true, and such an informative function of belief is not a matter of the number of individuals who hold the

32

belief, any more than it is a matter of the intensity with which they maintain the belief. One thing alone matters for Socrates: it is whether or not a belief is actually informed of the nature of the reality which the belief is assumed to interpret. When a belief is so informed, an individual who maintains the belief has knowledge.

Thus underlying the reflective life of Socrates is the faith that man can attain a trustworthy knowledge. The attainment of such knowledge presupposes that an individual can select from among beliefs the ones which are dependable, and the ones which are not. If such selection were not possible, there would be no justification to spend time appraising beliefs for their knowledge-value. But the appraisal of a belief on the basis of its informative function presupposes that one belief can be more informed than another. If this presupposition were not made, one belief would have as much significance for an individual as another belief.

But if there is one thing which Socrates refused to admit, it is that one belief has the same value as another belief, and that every belief has the same credentials. Socrates could not believe this and at the same time also spend his life in the search for beliefs which are more informed than other beliefs. The very selection from among beliefs expresses the conviction that there is a basis on which selection is justified.

If the only basis on which selection could be made were the number of people who hold a belief, the only method in moral philosophy would be the enumerative method. But the very fact that Socrates was interested in ascertaining the moral worth of beliefs implies that he had some standard by which to select from among beliefs the ones which he regarded as morally worthy. The very fact that he rejected some beliefs as morally unsatisfactory implies that he had some criterion of moral value with which he made the rejection. It is impossible to think about the moral significance of any belief unless one has some idea of what is morally worthy, in the sense of *worth one's approval*. Or, as Socrates himself says, "if we had no idea at all what virtue actually is, we could not possibly consult with anyone as to how he might best acquire it."[2]

The confidence that some patterns for living are worth more than others implies a criterion. The criterion is "what contributes to the worth of life." Although this criterion does not resolve all moral problems, it does, however, indicate the direction in which one must search for a resolution of the problems. One would have to search for an understanding of what is valuable in terms of life; and also for an understanding of which aspect of life is morally significant. When one has found this much, he then can evaluate beliefs in terms of their effectiveness for attaining the valued aspect of life. But until one knows what constitutes the worth of life, he cannot with any consistency select from among beliefs the ones which are informed recommendations how to attain the worth of life. This is not an insurmountable handicap to reflecting, but it does state one of the problems with which anyone will be confronted who tries to reflect upon the nature of life in an attempt to formulate a moral philosophy.

A moral philosophy can be formulated only when one has a basis for organizing ideas into a system. Yet, the very organization of such ideas is a selection; and such a selection is already the evaluation of ideas for their worth in such a system. Thus the very organization of ideas into a moral philosophy reveals an assumption about the justification for living. The way an individual interprets this moral end conditions what he selects as significant in life. Hence, a selection from among conventional practices, just as a selection from among beliefs, is an evaluation from the point of view of what one assumes constitutes the justification for living.

The conviction that an enlightenment of life is one justifica-

34

tion for living is a basic faith of Socrates. For Socrates, the very significance of human life is interpreted in terms of what is discovered in life which adds to the knowledge-content of life. Yet, it is obvious that an effort to learn is justified only if there is something which can be learned, otherwise such effort would be without purpose.

When Socrates declares that "every man is good in that wherein he is wise,"[3] he defines moral value in terms of knowledge. When one, for example, wants to know the nature of a morally praiseworthy courage, such as Socrates wanted to know in the *Laches,* he desires some form of knowledge. The specific knowledge one would have in this case would be, as Socrates says, "the knowledge of what *is* to be dreaded or dared, either in war or anything else." The apparently simple problem of defining "courage" thus turns out to be a very profound philosophical problem. It is profound for the very reason that Socrates is not interested only in knowing how some individuals propose to use words. He is not interested in a definition which is only an arbitrary agreement upon how a word is used. Knowing this much, and no more, would be merely an acquaintance with what people think. But Socrates is not interested in this.

He is interested in knowing the *warrant* for what people think. This very concern, therefore, means that he is not interested only in a semantic problem. He is not interested in knowing merely the agreement which people reach in the use of words in a language-context. He is interested rather in what one *must* know if he is to define a morally significant term in a manner that will be informed about a pattern of dependable living. Thus the interest of Socrates is in an ostensive definition; or better, in a proposition. A statement that courage is "knowledge of what *is* to be dreaded or dared" is a proposition. It is a statement about the conditions which must be fulfilled if one is to be *morally* courageous. Thus

35

this definition of courage is not purely verbal. It is not a proposal of how words are to be used in substitution for other words. It is rather a proposition which states what would have to be known *if* one were to become morally courageous.

This for some people may not appear to be saying very much, but it is, nevertheless, stating the moral problem, and it is stating it in terms of a moral task. One will, according to this statement, be in a position to say just what courage is only when he knows "what *is* to be dreaded and dared." The copula in this statement is not used with the sense of "means," as is the usage in a conventional definition. It is used here rather with the sense of an obligation. One would know the nature of courage only *if* he knew all that *should* be "dreaded or dared."

Socrates does not assume that he knows all that is to be dreaded, and all that is to be dared. His very unwillingness to claim that he has such knowledge makes the *Laches* a tentative dialogue. It is tentative in the sense that there is no detailed analysis of which conditions fulfill this definition of courage. The conclusion of the dialogue is a challenge to achieve such knowledge. One may know what he thinks is courage, but this is not the type of knowledge for which Socrates is in search. He is in search of an informed statement of what actually constitutes a pattern of life which takes into account all that *ought* to be dared, and all that *ought* to be endured. Thus the very desire to learn what this would be is the moral zeal with which Socrates reflects upon the problem. The conclusion of the dialogue is a recommendation. It is that "we ought all alike to seek out the best teacher we can find, for ourselves—for we need one—then for our boys . . . but to leave ourselves as we now are, this I do not advise."[4]

The conclusion is also a statement of faith. It is a declara-

36

tion that there is so much more to be known than one already knows that one underexploits the opportunities of his life when he does not earnestly take part in the search to know more than he already knows. The earnestness with which Socrates sustained this quest to learn is a testimony that he believed that there is more to learn than he already knew. He likewise was not satisfied with the indolence so common in life to accept all that is claimed as knowledge as if it were knowledge. He was interested rather to ascertain the very *warrant* for the knowledge-claims, in order to find out, if possible, whether what people assume to be knowledge actually is knowledge.

Knowledge is information. It is not what someone thinks is information. So likewise, what actually constitutes courage is not necessarily what someone may think it is; and it may not even be what most people think it is. The problem for a reflectively earnest individual is to find out the very warrant for what people think. The warrant for thinking is a norm to which thinking must conform *if* it is to be informed.

A claim to knowledge is a proposition which one affirms because he believes it to be informed. But to believe that a proposition is an informed interpretation is not necessarily to have knowledge. Only the possession of an informed interpretation is knowledge. This is the theory of knowledge which is presupposed by Socrates. It is, however, not developed into a systematic theory for the very reason that Socrates was not concerned in formulating a theory of knowledge; as if this were the most urgent need in his life. He was interested above all else in pioneering the way in which reflection *should be* conducted in acquiring morally significant knowledge.

Basic to the moral philosophy of Socrates is the faith that morally valuable patterns for living can be discovered; and so morally valuable principles can be formulated. Hence the recurring thesis of Socrates: "Thus equipped, the human race would indeed act and live according to knowledge."[5] This is a faith. It is the faith that when an individual possesses knowledge of what he ought to do, his life will have the benefit of a directing, ordering principle.

A reflection upon a moral problem leads from one problem to another. This is just what Socrates endeavors to make clear in his teaching. The very difficulty of the reflective inquiry is itself what made people annoyed with him, and he cites such an annoyance of his contemporaries as the real reason underlying his condemnation. One need not have a faith equal to the faith of Socrates to be able to respect Socrates; but he does have to have respect for a life motivated by faith, or he would never respect Socrates. The life of Socrates is motivated by a faith that there is more to be known than is already known; and this faith defines for him the very program of his life, which is a search for such *knowledge-yet-to-be*.

The driving motive in the life of Socrates is the conviction that the value of life itself depends upon searching for what can be known. It is the belief that knowledge is "the noblest thing in the world."[6] But the noblest thing in the world is itself a norm. It is a standard of value. It is not only what is valued by men. Ideas which are assumed to be informed are regarded by individuals as knowledge, but their classification as such is only a claim to knowledge. This raises not only the question of what must be known in order to be informed, but also the question of what must be known in order to make any competent evaluations. This then is a question of what type of knowledge is worth having; and this is the question which Socrates as a moral philosopher constantly asks.

The formulation of this problem is the rich contribution of Socrates to morally earnest life. It is not a simple rule of the thumb which can be known with a little effort so that one has the comfortable assurance that he has learned all that he ought to know. The very awareness of what it means to be enlightened is an awareness of a responsibility. The moral responsibility is to know all that one must know in order to be informed of all that his life can become. This is the meaning of the inscription on the Delphic temple which Socrates regarded as the fundamental moral obligation. It is to "know thyself." But in the attempt to know one's self, one must be informed of all that *should* enter into his reflective awareness. This is indeed a task, and so a challenge. The very scope of the task is enough to enable one to understand why Socrates believed that he had to give up all other occupations in life in order to spend time in this single task. Whether or not this may be driving a point too far is certainly a problem with which everyone is confronted who evaluates the merit of the life of Socrates.

If what is *believed* to be knowledge were the norm of what justifies all learning-effort, then life could be justified on any level. But if moral philosophy is not to pass into a justification for doing what is done, and for knowing what is believed to be knowledge, then a criterion very different from an individual's belief must be proposed as the norm of moral responsibility. Moral responsibility for Socrates is knowing. It is knowing all that *ought to be known*. This basic moral conviction affirms the faith that human life can become enlightened. This is the faith of Socrates. That moral responsibility involves such enlightening, and may even be defined in terms of it, is also the faith of Socrates. This faith is the profound contribution of Socrates to the history of moral philosophy and to human life. Without this faith, there would be no earnest and sustained reflective search, out of which an adequate moral philosophy may emerge. Socrates thus is a witness to one of the indispensable conditions for moral philosophy. It is a faith that an earnest search for morally significant knowledge is justified, because such knowledge can be acquired.

2. *The philosophy of the Sophists*

The philosophical significance of the faith of Socrates cannot be appreciated until one understands what a philosophy without faith actually is. Such a philosophy without faith was a popular point of view of the day in which Socrates lived. It was the teaching of the Sophists. What Socrates found objectionable in their sophistication is its offensive dogmatism. It would, in fact, be difficult to conceive a more dogmatic attitude toward philosophy itself than characterizes the point of view of the Sophists. For the Sophists everything is clear, and yet, the very clarity of their analyses of all philosophical problems discloses how simple-minded some sophistication can be. Thinking that the clarity of their analyses is an index to the *adequacy* of their interpretations, they were unaware of the very problems which perplexed Socrates.

The philosophy of the Sophist is clear, concise, and confidently dogmatic. According to one of the Sophists, Thrasymachus, there is only one principle which needs to be understood if one is to understand the nature of all morally significant distinctions. It is that the clever individual is the most successful in life; and what he does for his own advantage is what is right for him to do. The problem which perplexed Socrates, however, was to ascertain what is the *right* thing to believe in order to do what is *right*. For the Sophist Thrasymachus, however, this is no problem. What one is shrewd enough to do in taking advantage of people is a mark of his superiority. Such superiority of one over another is construed as an index of an individual's "right" to have what he is unscrupulous enough to get. The transition in the thinking of Thrasymachus from "success in taking advantage of" to "the superiority of the individual who takes such advantage," easily

40

passes into the doctrine that "the one who can take such advantage is superior." He is superior in the sense that he can do what another does not do; and so, from the obvious fact that one without scruples can take advantage of another who refuses to act unscrupulously, it follows for Thrasymachus, that the one who takes advantage, because limited by no considerations for the rights of another, becomes the norm itself of what is right. This line of reasoning is perfectly clear, and an example of it has been recorded in the first book of the *Republic*: "In private contracts; whenever the unjust is the partner of the just, you will find . . . the unjust man has always more and the just less."[7] He cites this perfectly obvious fact as sufficient evidence that what one can do is a mark of his superiority over another who does not do the same thing.

That this type of argument could even have emerged into the semblance of a system of moral philosophy indicates something of the level of life with which Socrates was confronted in working out his own moral philosophy. From the point of view of Thrasymachus, Socrates is naïve to believe that there is merit in respecting another's rights. From this point of view, another's rights are simply what he can manage to maintain after an unscrupulous individual gets done with him. The more one can get, the more he vindicates his "rights;" and the more he affirms such "rights," the more he demonstrates his superiority to claim them.

There is no way to break the logical consistency of this argument. Although the premise of the argument may be as perverse as any can be, still when one thinks logically within the scope of this premise, he derives a system as logically consistent as it is morally perverse. Hence, when the development of a systematic point of view is regarded as evidence for the intellectual skill of an individual, and such skill is construed as a superiority to the abilities of all who do not develop the same air-tight system, there is no way to cite a standard by which the skill itself may be evaluated for its moral significance. The very skill to formulate a system of ideas within the limits of any premise is construed by a Sophist to be a mark of intellectual superiority. Hence, when a Sophist contrasts himself with a person such as Socrates, he comes out confirmed in the soundness of his assumption. He is aware that when one has a clearly stated premise, an entire system of philosophy logically emerges; whereas, when one is earnestly searching to find a worthy premise, he has no logically comparable system. Thus by contrast, the searching Socrates stands in the shadow of the luminous Thrasymachus, for whom everything in life is clear. All behavior may be evaluated by one principle: what an individual can get is what he is entitled to; and he is entitled to it by virtue of his ability to get it. Such ability is his superiority, and hence the superior individual is he who has a right to take what he has the ability to get.

One may go round and round with this statement, and the very circularity seems to confirm it. Assuming that a restatement of a premise is the confirmation of the premise, Thrasymachus saw no basis on which another premise could be defended. But the very difference between Socrates and Thrasymachus is the attitude toward the philosophical significance of a clearly stated premise. That the idea of Thrasymachus is clear can hardly be disputed. The very fact that it is clear makes discussion about it possible. The long discussions which Socrates had with the Sophists are indications that Socrates was satisfied with the clarity of their ideas. But the discussions continued for many years just because Socrates was convinced that the clarity of an idea is not a *sufficient* credential of its adequacy. He was convinced that an idea may be clear, and yet morally deceptive. Thus, Socrates never confused the criteria of logic with the criteria of moral adequacy.

The moral criterion which Socrates sought was the adequacy

42

of a view in terms of its contribution to the enhancement of human life—which means a life in a social situation. Thus Socrates was not interested in finding out how to state a clear principle which would ignore the fact that an individual's advantage is not to be contrasted with the advantage of others. This very conviction is the faith of Socrates, and with this faith, he debated with the Sophists. But Thrasymachus has no such faith, and yet, the poverty of his faith constitutes the limits within which he proposes to formulate a moral philosophy.

The very scope of a moral philosophy is set for an individual by his belief about what is significant. For Thrasymachus there is only one significant factor: it is what he can get, provided he wants it. Thus desire is for him the one supremely significant factor in formulating a moral principle. For him there are no considerations to be taken into account of the effect of one's actions upon others. Thrasymachus is not interested in the problems of a citizen, because a citizen, from his point of view, is simply an individual who knows what he wants, when he wants it, and knows nothing whatsoever about the limitations to which his desires ought to conform. There is no *ought* in contrast to desire. Hence, he assumes that what an individual can get is what he is entitled to, and what he gets, demonstrates his superiority; and his superiority is his right to have what he gets. The argument may go on and on, but it is the same thing no matter how long it is extended. He defines an individual's rights in terms of what he does; and what he does shows what he can do. What he can do is his strength; his virtue; his superiority to another who does not do what he himself does; and the inference, of course, is that the other doesn't do it because he can't do it; and he can't do it because he is inferior.

Thrasymachus is a perfect example of a clever tongue, arguing from a perverse premise. This is a common combi-

nation, and what makes it so morally repugnant is that the
very skill in argument is assumed by such an individual to be
an indication of his superiority. There is, however, no way
that one can out-argue such an individual. The very attempt
to do so is construed by him as the mark of naïveté not to see
the invincibility of the argument.

With this single premise, Thrasymachus assumes that he
explains away every moral perplexity which Socrates proposes as a problem for serious reflection. According to Thrasymachus, there is only one thing that one needs to know: it is to
find out how to get what one wants, when he wants it, without raising any question of the consequences of his acts in
terms of other individuals' lives, and in terms of the State.
"In their dealings with the State when there is an income
tax, (one) will pay more and (another) less on the same
amount of income." The reason for this, according to Thrasymachus, is clear: the one who pays more is the unfortunate
one. He is the one whom people call "just." The one who pays
less to the State, however, and so has more for himself, is the
so-called "unjust" man. But from the point of view of Thrasymachus, the unjust "is the happiest of men, and those who
refuse to do injustice are the most miserable."[3] This conclusion
follows from the premise. There is one and only one thing
which an individual needs to take into account in what he
does: it is what he himself wants, when he wants it. This is
his right. His right is what he can get by any means.

When one begins with such a point of view, there is no way
to persuade him by argument that he is mistaken. His confidence in his premise is fortified by the very fact that one
cannot logically discredit it. What he infers from it is what
is implied in it; and this is sound logic. One can ask nothing
more in the name of logic than consistency with a given
premise; and yet, asking no more than this in a moral philosophy is just the mark of the Sophist.

Thrasymachus knew contemporary philosophy, and he knew which philosophical authority to cite to corroborate his own point of view. It was the theory of knowledge as stated by Protagoras. Protagoras maintained that an individual can know nothing other than his own experience. Unable to know anything other than his own experience, he has no justification for searching for a principle to which he ought to conform. The desire to find such a principle, however, was the motivating drive in the life of Socrates. But from the point of view of Protagoras, the very search of Socrates reveals his naïve theory of knowledge. Socrates assumed that there is something other than an individual's experience, a knowledge of which constitutes the objective of an individual's search; and he believed that it is an individual's obligation to know all that he can of such a reality. But when one begins with the premise of Protagoras that one can know nothing other than his own experience, he would, if he could think consistently, realize that it would be a waste of time to try to know something other than his experience. Thus a theory of knowledge sets limits to a moral philosophy. No one with intelligence enough to think clearly would try to know what his theory of knowledge affirms cannot be known.

The theory of knowledge as maintained by Protagoras is a radical empiricism. Such a point of view is that the only reality which an individual can know is his own experience. When one begins with such a point of view, he already has a moral philosophy. It is that whatever can be known as a principle for living is limited to what one can discover within his own experiences; and the scope of this search is always limited to what an individual assumes he knows. There is, therefore, no challenge, as there is for Socrates, to discover the moral significance of a reality other than one's own experience.

Protagoras' theory of knowledge likewise implies a theory of value. It is that there is one norm of value: it is what an individual believes is valuable. As a theory of value, this becomes the well-known dictum of Protagoras: "Man is the measure of all things."[9] This *homo mensura* doctrine, which constitutes the basic premise of his theory of knowledge; his theory of value; and his moral philosophy, was not pulled out of thin air as an independent premise. From the point of view of Protagoras, it is an implication of another point of view. It is the logical consequence of what was regarded as an incontestable theory of reality; and this theory of reality is the materialistic philosophy of Democritus.

Democritus believed that *everything* can be explained in terms of matter, which consists of atoms without qualities, which differ only in geometrical features, such as shape, size, and position. When this theory of reality, therefore, becomes the basic premise with which a philosophical psychology is constructed, it means that experience must be interpreted in terms of material atoms making an impact upon one another. An individual's experiences are the activities of material atoms; and an individual's body defines the limits for *his* experiences. There is no action at a distance.[10] There are only the impacts of bodies upon each other; and the medium in which such impacts occur must itself be material. Hence what is ordinarily called "mental life," or "consciousness," is one type of activity of material organization. When one maintains that *all* reality can be interpreted in terms of the impact of material atoms upon each other, then one must formulate a moral philosophy within these limits. This is just what the Sophists did. And they did this because they assumed that Democritus had formulated an incontestable point of view. Diogenes Laertius declares that "the public deemed him worthy of the honour paid to a god."[11] Sextus Empiricus likewise declares that the voice of Democritus "has been compared to the voice of God."[12] One does not have to be very imaginative to understand why the Sophists, as contemporaries of Democritus, should reflect the implications of his metaphysic. When any one is regarded as "omniscient;" as "worthy of the honour paid to a god;" and is even compared "to the voice of God," it is obvious that what is thought by all who pay such respects will, in so far as they can understand, be in conformity to his teachings. People, says Aristotle, "take the mould of the characteristics they approve."[13] One cannot, therefore, understand the hold which the Sophists had upon the Athenians at the time of Socrates without understanding the philosophical authority which the Sophists themselves cited for their beliefs. The moral philosophy of the Sophists is not spun out of thin air; and it does not rest upon an independent premise. It is very much a part of the point of view of the times—of the philosophy of reality which the intellectuals took for granted.

When, however, it is taken for granted that all experience must be interpreted in terms of the activity of material atoms, then it is also obvious that no experiences have informative significance of a reality external to experiences themselves. They are results of the impacts of atoms; and what is transmitted are only the impacts. This means that what an individual knows are his own experiences, and *nothing more*.[14]

This is the conclusion which the Sophist Gorgias drew, and it is a logically implied conclusion from the premise as stated by Democritus. One cannot know that anything exists external to his own experiences; and "if anything did exist we could not know it;" and "if perchance a man should come to know it, it would remain a secret, he would be unable to describe it to his fellowmen." He would be unable to describe it for the very reason that his language is his own experience, and another individual who interprets his language would in turn be confined to his own experience. Thus, even if an individual might possess some information on the basis of an analysis of his own experience, he would not be justified in assuming this information could be transmitted. Again, the vast difference of Socrates and Gorgias. Gorgias believed that an individual can *not* know more than his own experience. Socrates believed that an individual *can* know more than his own experience. He believed that although whatever is known is always within the limits set by one's capacities for experience, still what is known is not necessarily only experience itself. It is possible to know a pattern of living by which one may be wisely directed.

Thus the very moral philosophies of Socrates and the Sophist Gorgias could not be farther apart for the very reason that their theories of knowledge are radically different; and their theories of knowledge are different because they begin with radically different theories of the nature of experiences. But again, their theories of experience differ because their metaphysics differ. The very search of Socrates for a principle which is adequate to be the authority of human life rests upon a theory of reality and a theory of knowledge which differ radically from the theories of the Sophists Thrasymachus, Protagoras, and Gorgias.

3. *The pessimism, cynicism, and nihilism of the Sophists*

One needs only intelligence enough to understand language to realize the full significance of Democritus' premise for moral philosophy. A metaphysic which affirms that *all* reality consists of atoms which differ only in "size and shape"[15] also affirms that whatever else is thought to be other than such geometrical properties is other than the real. If "*the* principle of *all* things" is matter; and if the properties of matter are exclusively geometrical; then *everything* which is other than the geometrical features of matter is non-essential, or accidental. From the single explanatory principle of the materialistic metaphysic of Democritus it follows that all ex-

perience—and this includes all knowing, or all claims to knowledge—must be accounted for in terms of the activity of material organizations. Sensations, therefore, are not informative
of material organizations: they are the impacts of one material
organization upon another. Hence, from the metaphysical
principle that "magnitudes or atoms constitute reality"[16] it
follows, by the simplest inference, that sensory experiences do
not inform an individual of any reality external to himself.
It therefore is not an incidental figure of speech which Democritus uses when he says that "the senses are not dim but
blind." If they were *dim,* it would at least suggest that in
some small measure they might be informative of a reality
external to an individual's own body. But the only inference
which is logically permissible from the metaphysical premise
as stated by Democritus is that *all* experiences are only activities occurring in the impacts of one material organization
upon another. This means for a theory of knowledge that no
experience has informative function.

By this definition of reality, experiences do not inform an
individual of anything other than the notions which he himself entertains. The informative function of experience is
denied by the very premise with which Democritus constructs
his metaphysic. One problem of philosophy, however, is to
account for claims to knowledge; and Democritus declares
that it is "by convention colour exists," "but in reality atoms
and void."[17] Convention here means opinions without *any* informative significance. This is the inference of Galen, who, in
interpreting the position of Democritus, points out that the
"phrase 'by convention' means the same thing as 'by custom,'
and 'for us,' not according to the nature of things themselves,
which he calls 'in reality,' coining the term from 'real' which
means 'true.' " No clearer analysis of a theory of knowledge
as implied in any metaphysic could be stated. This explanation for all qualitative distinctions, hence all values, logically

follows from the very statement that all reality consists of atoms which "have no qualities."

One needs no more philosophical ability than an understanding of the use of language to understand what theory of knowledge is implied in the metaphysic of Democritus; and one needs no peculiar philosophical attitude to know just what theory of value is likewise implied in his metaphysic. All judgments of value-distinctions are conventions; and conventions are customs. Customs in turn have no foundation in informed interpretations of the nature of reality. They are purely accidental; and this is just what the Sophists maintained about all value-distinctions. All moral judgments for the Sophists are customs; and all customs are accidental developments in a particular culture.

The Sophists could think. That is just what constituted the *logically* unassailable character of their philosophy. They cited Democritus; and it was Democritus whom people accepted as the "voice of God." With such an estimate of Democritus, it follows that from the point of view of the Sophists, they were the *logically* sound interpreters of the nature of moral values. This transition is obvious; and it has been obvious to everyone in the history of philosophy who took the statements of Democritus at their full face value. Diogenes and Galen point out how the theory of values basic to the philosophy of the Sophists follows from the definition of reality as material organizations whose properties are quantitative. Thus Diogenes states the implication: "The qualities of things exist merely by convention; in nature there is nothing but atoms and void space."[18] Every value judgment which is affirmed by an individual about morally significant distinctions is, therefore, only a statement of preference. It is not a statement about the nature of any essential, or fundamental, difference whose very difference in *significance for living* is its nature as a moral principle. There are no such principles except merely by convention. Hence, no belief can be informed about a real superiority of one principle to another.

There are no essential differences in principles for living when reality is defined as Democritus defines it. It is simply playing fast and loose with language to read the metaphysic of Democritus without also understanding exactly which theory of knowledge; theory of values; and hence moral philosophy, is already implied. From the definition of reality as given by Democritus, it follows that there is no true guidance which can be discovered in life. Sextus Empiricus points out that Democritus "flatly denies truth exists."[19] Yet, if there are no fundamental differences in the merit of types of living, then any loyalty of an individual to one principle in preference to another is uninformed enthusiasm. Believing as Democritus does about the nature of reality, one likewise must have a very definite belief about the warrant for all human earnestness expressed in the loyalties of human life to principles. What Democritus believes is stated by one of the ancients: he "ridiculed everything as if all human interests were ridiculous."[20] Such a disparagement of human earnestness in search of a principle to which one may with justification give the allegiance of his life is what would follow from the theory of value as is implied in the theory of reality stated by Democritus. Thus what is thought about man, and about his activities, including his loyalties and his devotions, is already implied in what is thought about reality, when the interpretation of reality is a metaphysic, or a doctrine about *all* reality. If one understands what the term *all* means, he then understands just what Democritus proposes to explain by means of his principle. Included in *all* is human life. Included in human life are the value-distinctions which are basic to moral judgments. But, if all distinctions of value are only custom, and custom is *by definition* not informed of reality, then no value-distinctions are interpretations of reality. They are

51

purely accidents. This is just what every Sophist maintained.

The Sophist contemporaries of Socrates accepted the premise of Democritus as defining the scope within which *everything* was to be interpreted. Thus a moral philosophy which interprets the nature of value-distinctions is, for the Sophists, a theory about purely accidental points of view. According to them, there can be no informed beliefs about the superior worth of a principle in terms of its suitability or adequacy for human life. All human beliefs are of equal truth-character. One Sophist maintained that all beliefs are true. Another maintained that no beliefs are true. The significance of these positions for a moral philosophy is the same. If there are no criteria by which the soundness or the warrant for any beliefs can be measured, then there are no beliefs which are more worthy to be accepted as principles for living than other beliefs. This is the clearest possible statement of cynicism in moral philosophy. Cynicism is the disparagement of *all* reflective effort to discover, or to formulate, a principle which is the most worthy pattern by which one ought to live. Understanding what Democritus affirmed about reality, the Sophists were already cynical about all earnest effort to discover such a principle which is more suitable for life than other principles. All principles are accidents of belief.

It is not just by chance that the Sophists, therefore, are cynical about human efforts, and cynical about the nature of earnest life in search of principles. They are cynics about such searching for the very reason that they are sceptical about the possibility of knowing such principles. Their attitude toward earnest life is the nature of cynicism. Cynicism is not a theory of reality. It is an attitude toward human life which has a theory of reality that is cited as the justification for morally earnest effort.

But the Cynic's defense of his attitude rests upon a theory of reality. No philosophy can be formulated without a theory of reality, although a cynic would not be consistent if he were to spend much time formulating a theory of reality. The Cynic assumes himself to be enlightened; and his enlightenment, from his point of view, consists in his knowledge that there is no warrant for an earnest effort to discover one principle of life which ought to be respected rather than another. There is no "ought" in the sense of a norm by means of which one's life may become enlightened the more one knows the norm. The very distinction, therefore, which Socrates made between what he *assumes to know* and the norm of *what would constitute knowledge,* is a distinction which is depreciated by the Sophist; and the very depreciation of this faith of Socrates is what makes a sophist also a cynic. He is contemptuous of the earnestness with which anyone labors to know more than he already knows. The Cynic depreciates this type of life because he regards the goal of such a life to be a fiction. The very classification of all goals in life as fictions is, of course, itself a theory of reality. Thus even a cynic has a philosophy. It may not be a very developed one. It couldn't be; since the very development of a consistent, well-thought-out point of view is the product of effort; and a consistent cynic doesn't believe that effort for such a purpose is justified.

A cynic, therefore, is one whose life is intellectually paralyzed; and yet, he has sufficient interest to rationalize his intellectual indolence. This is no contradiction. It is just a fact of human life that some individuals do not find the effort to sustain thinking congenial to their indolence. They take over philosophies, and with these appropriated philosophies they dogmatically disparage the efforts to philosophize.

It would be senseless to classify Democritus as a cynic towards philosophy. His philosophy is one of the monumental achievements of the human intellect. But his zeal to sustain thinking sufficiently to formulate a metaphysic is incongruous with his own theory of values. He believed that the effort to think is justified, because in thinking about the nature of reality one can distinguish false ideas from true ideas. Yet, the theory of knowledge which is implied in his metaphysic is contradictory to the theory of knowledge which justifies his philosophical thinking. It is, however, a common fact that there are individuals who earnestly work out philosophies which include premises that discredit the very justification for their effort. The philosophy of Democritus is one such philosophy. Democritus believed that there is a difference between superstition and enlightenment. This difference consists in knowing the nature of reality in contrast to having erroneous ideas about it. But, the premise that all value-distinctions are only customs implies that this distinction between sound philosophy and mythology is only a convention; a custom; an accidental, and therefore, an unjustified distinction.

One of the requirements for a consistent philosophy is that its premises should not repudiate the very justification for formulating a philosophy. The Cynic cannot formulate a philosophy without contradicting himself. Democritus did contradict himself; but the contradiction did not discourage him from thinking, since living without thinking was not congenial to him.

Chapter Three

MORAL PHILOSOPHY AND A THEORY
OF KNOWLEDGE

1. *A moral philosophy is formulated within the presuppositions of a theory of knowledge*

Whatever one may reasonably think about the nature of moral principles is logically implied in his general theory of knowledge. One, therefore, who is able to think consistently cannot go very far in formulating a moral philosophy without revealing his theory of knowledge. No matter what one's vocabulary may be, and no matter how he may state his moral philosophy, it is impossible to conceal his theory of knowledge. This is one aspect of philosophy which discloses itself on every turn. This fact becomes obvious when one examines any well-thought-out position, as for example, a modern existentialist's philosophy.

The very manner in which Karl Jaspers interprets the significance of Plato's philosophy reveals Jaspers' own theory of knowledge. He maintains that "Plato teaches the eternal, fundamental experiences of philosophy."[1] This is certainly true: Plato's philosophy is an example of thinking; and hence it is an instance of philosophical experience. But it may be pointed out that Plato was not primarily interested in formulating a philosophy as a type of experience. He was concerned to formulate a way of living by means of which one could be directed to know a reality other than experience. Yet, from the point of view of Jaspers, nothing can be known of a reality other than experience. Hence, what Jaspers regards as philosophically significant in Plato's thinking is the philosophizing experience itself. This is obvious when he declares that "The essential is the operation of transcending."[2] By this he means that in Plato's philosophy there is a reference beyond what has already been thought. This reference is a type of experience. He therefore maintains that the contribution of Plato to the history of philosophy, and to moral philosophy in particular, is the searching, which is a transcending reference within life. But, it must be emphasized that the reference is not to a reality external to experience. Experience is what is known; and the experience itself is what is cultivated as the most significant thing in Plato's philosophizing. "In the study of Plato," Jaspers maintains, "we obtain no fixed knowledge but learn to philosophize for ourselves."[3]

One certainly must agree with Jaspers that the only way to appreciate the nature of the experience which constitutes Plato's philosophizing is to study Plato's philosophy. But, it must also be stressed that Plato's motive in philosophizing may be interpreted very differently than it is interpreted by Jaspers. It may be interpreted as an attempt to know a reality other than experience, by which one's life may be informed. Yet, this very interpretation is unwarranted from the point of view of Jaspers. Jaspers' theory of knowledge discredits the assumption that information of a reality transcendent of human life is possible. According to him, "whatever we know is only a beam of light cast by our interpretation into being."[4] It follows that Plato's interpretation informs us only of Plato's experience. It reveals to us a type of experience which characterizes an individual who strives to learn. Such striving is a transcend*ing* reference internal to experience. Thus, in a study of what Plato has written, one is not given information about a reality which Plato interprets. He is informed about the interpreting efforts of Plato. According to Jaspers, Plato's philosophy enables us to understand what constitutes the nature of a life which strives to learn, and in striving is referred beyond what is already regarded as knowledge.

Jaspers believes that the scope of possible knowledge is limited to experience. This is the Kantian theory of knowledge which he takes for granted. He declares that "The phenomenality of the empirical world was made fully clear by Kant."[5] If one can understand terminology in philosophy, he certainly knows what Jaspers maintains about the nature of knowing, and about the nature of what can be known. Phenomena, according to Kant, are organized experiences. What is known when such organized experiences are analyzed is not only particular experiences; but also organizing forms; and these forms are informative of the organizing capacities of the interpreter. Hence, when such forms are known, nothing is known about any reality transcendent of, or external to, experience. Whatever, therefore, may be claimed as warranted knowledge is, from the point of view of Kant, an understanding of experience: it is not an understanding of the nature of any reality external to experience. This is also the assumption basic to Jaspers' theory of knowledge.

A philosophy, however, is often interpreted by individuals who read into it their own points of view. Thus, when Jaspers speaks of "the subject-object dichotomy" as a "basic condition of our thinking,"[6] some may assume that Jaspers speaks about an object other than self. He, however, does nothing of the sort. The distinction of subject and object is internal to experience. It is a distinction by the individual; and what is distinguished are experiences. No knowledge whatsoever is claimed of a reality external to experience. What is known is "phenomenon; not a thing in itself."

The very terminology "thing in itself" is, however, one

of the straw men in philosophical contests, and around this concept possibly more energy has been senselessly expended than around any other fiction. If by "thing in itself" one means a reality which is not interpreted by an individual, then obviously no one ever has had, or ever will have, an informative experience of such a reality. This follows simply from the way it is defined. *If,* however, there is a reality other than an individual's interpretation, it is possible that his interpretation may be informed of its nature.

An interpretation is an individual's experience. But the informative character of it is determined by what is known of a reality which is interpreted. The position, however, that every interpretation is always from the point of view of an interpreter, and therefore is not informative of any reality other than the interpreter himself is also a perfectly clear point of view. Thus, there are two points of view; and they constitute the basic premises of two fundamentally different theories of knowledge. For any one to propose that he *knows* which one of the two is *the* right view is certainly as obvious a dogmatism as can be found. But, if one maintains that within experience it *may* be possible to know something of a reality other than experience, then one may assume that some experiences *may* be informative of such a reality transcendent of experience. Yet, it is this very possibility which is denied by Kant; and hence the theory of knowledge which Jaspers presupposes likewise denies such a possibility. This means that the objects about which Jaspers speaks are distinctions within experience. The "subject-object dichotomy" is such a distinction. The transcend*ing* reference is another such distinction within experience. Whatever there may be transcend*ent* of experience, in the sense of existing apart from experience, is "not an object for a subject." Hence, "it is beyond cognition." "Everything that is an object for us reveals to us its phenomenality in contrast to its being-in-itself."

It would be impossible to make any distinction in a philosophy clearer than this. The initial premise in Jaspers' theory of knowledge is perfectly clear. It is that the object of knowledge is experience. This means that we are aware only of distinctions internal to our experiences. When one assumes that this is *the only* warranted theory of knowledge, he likewise interprets the philosophical significance of all philosophies from this point of view. What can be known when we understand the theology as written by St. Augustine is, according to Jaspers, the searching soul of St. Augustine. He declares that "Augustine's works remain to this day a spring from which all thinkers draw who seek to know the soul in its depths."[7]

But, mistaken or not mistaken, Augustine did not believe that he was writing only a psychology or a philosophy of a searching soul. He proposed to interpret the nature of divine reality transcendent of human life, which he assumed can be known in the searching life. What Jaspers regards as the religious significance of St. Augustine's theory is the account of St. Augustine's search. Important as this may be, it still is not what St. Augustine regarded as the significance of his theology. From Augustine's point of view, the theology which he formulated is an instructive set of interpretations of the nature of the divine reality. With his interpretation, he believed that man would know more of the nature of the divine reality than without the interpretations as he articulated them into a theology. Basic to the writings of St. Augustine is the faith that there is "A Wisdom which needing no light, enlightens the minds that need it."[8] St. Augustine believed this Wisdom to be transcendent of all human life; and he believed that it is the one completely dependable source for the enlightenment of life. Hence, the objective of human life, according to St. Augustine, is to know this reality which is transcendent of human life. But for Jaspers, the objective of all philosophy is to know the nature of the self. "Philosophy concerns man as man."[9]

The significant aspect of an individual's life, according to Jaspers, is his decisions: "a decision with which I myself am identical."[10] Decisions, however, differ in their character. Some decisions are uncompromising. In other words, they are "unconditional." Such unconditional decisions are the most significant events in an individual's life. They constitute the "fulfilled" life. "Just as trees sink their roots deeply and grow high in the air, so is the fulfilled man rooted in the unconditional; all others are like shrubs which can be pulled up and transplanted."[11] The key word in this statement is "the unconditional." The frequent citation of Jaspers' position within some Protestant theological discussions reveals, however, that it is this very word which is misunderstood. Some assume that Jaspers speaks about a reality transcendent of human life which is the "unconditional" reality which one ought to know. But this interpretation could not be more incompatible with the philosophy of Jaspers. The "unconditional" is not a feature of a reality transcendent of human experience. It is a type of experience. Just as "transcending" is a type of experience, so is "the unconditional" a type of experience. It is the type of experience which occurs in an individual "as opposed to passive acceptance of things as they are."[12] The uncompromising unwillingness to accept what is as if it were all one might experience is "the unconditional *attitude*."[13] One cannot point out too vigorously that the unconditional for Jaspers is an attitude. It is a feature of experience, or a type of experience.

Thus, using the same terms as are commonly used in the history of the Christian Church, such as "unconditional" and "transcending," some readers take for granted that Jaspers speaks about an unconditioned reality transcendent of human life. Jaspers, however, says nothing about a reality transcendent of human experience. The unconditional is an attitude; and "the unconditional attitude implies a decision."[14] The "unconditional" for Jaspers is a type of experience; a type of living: or a character of life. "As opposed to passive acceptance of things as they are, the unconditional attitude implies a decision . . . a decision with which I myself am identical."[15]

Yet, this very explanation adds confusion to philosophically uncritical readers. The unconditional as Jaspers uses the term, does not designate a reality transcendent of experience. Authentic being is the individual whose decisions are unconditional. This is not only implied in his theory of knowledge: it is also explicitly stated, and can readily be understood by anyone who does not read into Jaspers' terms what Jaspers himself does not. Jaspers declares that "to partake in the eternal, in being . . . implies absolute reliability and loyalty, which derive not from nature but from our decisions."[16] The term "decision" is the critical word here. It offers the key to an understanding of Jaspers' use of the words "eternal;" "in being;" "absolute reliability." "Absolute reliability," according to Jaspers, is "the unconditional." The unconditional, however, is not a reality transcendent of an individual's life. It is an uncompromising decision.

Hence, following Kant, Jaspers likewise maintains that there is no unconditional imperative which an individual can know that is other than what is internal to his own experience. "The unconditional imperative comes to me as the command of my authentic self to my mere empirical existence."[17] This distinction of "authentic self" and "empirical existence" may be regarded by some readers as a distinction between experience and a reality other than experience. But no such distinction is made by Jaspers. The unconditional is the decision with which an individual completely identifies himself: it is his "authentic self." The "authentic self" is the individual whose decisions are unconditional: they are not conditioned

61

by conventions, and what others may think. "We are conscious of our freedom when we recognize imperatives addressed to us. It is up to us whether we carry them out or evade them."[18]

This, however, is what any one might say who formulates a moral philosophy: it is the individual who makes his own decisions, and if his decisions are to be *his own* acts, they cannot be coerced, or forced, by factors external to himself. "We cannot seriously deny that we make a decision, by which we decide concerning ourselves, and that we are responsible."[19] Such deciding is freedom. According to Jaspers, therefore, what is most important to an individual who is striving for selfhood, or freedom, is not a scriptural commandment, even though it may be designated "a commandment of God." The very term "God" as used by Jaspers may itself be misleading to an individual who reads Jaspers' statement that "Freedom and God are inseparable."[20]

It might be assumed that Jaspers maintains that a divine reality transcendent of human life is a condition essential for freedom in life. But this is not Jaspers' position: it is reading into Jaspers' philosophy a traditional Christian belief. Jaspers maintains "The voice of God lies in the self-awareness that dawns in the individual;"[21] and "the voice of God" of which Jaspers here speaks is not an authority for life which has an independent status external to life. Nothing here is claimed about "the voice of God" which is transcendent of an individual's experience. The individual's experience is "the voice of God:" "The voice of God lies in the self-awareness that dawns in the individual, when he is open to everything that comes to him from his tradition and environment."[22] Jaspers does not say that an awareness of "the voice of God" "dawns in the individual." "The voice of God" *lies in the self-awareness,* or consists in that type of life in which an individual "is open to everything that comes to him from his tradition and environment."

"The highest freedom is experienced in freedom from the world, and this freedom is a profound bond with transcendence."[23] This does not affirm that an individual's freedom is in relation to a reality transcendent of human life. Of such a reality, nothing, according to Jaspers, can be known. An individual has immediate awareness of his own freedom. Such freedom is the transcendence, or the referring of an individual beyond all imposed requirements to the responsibility which he himself imposes upon himself. This is freedom, as Jaspers uses the term. Such freedom is inseparable from God, because godhead is a quality of an individual's own life. "Philosophy . . . relates itself directly to godhead."[24] This means that the searching of an individual to find himself, which is his authentic being, is itself the type of experience which is the level of god.

Jaspers maintains that "Any restriction on man's freedom, created by God and oriented toward God, is a restriction upon the very thing through which God manifests himself."[25] Although Jaspers uses the term "God," what he means by "God" is, however, radically different from a reality transcendent of man, and yet knowable by him to the extent that he conditions his life to enable him to know its nature. Thus, if the same statement were to be made without the term "God," it would become apparent to everyone that the position in no way has any similarity whatsoever to the position in the Fourth Gospel that "to all who received him . . . he gave power to become children of God, who were born, not . . . of the will of man, but of God."[26] Jaspers maintains that an individual would not be morally free if *any* reality external to him were to be a factor in determining his decisions.

The terminology of Jaspers, therefore, may be misleading

to some. Its meaning becomes clear, however, when one constantly recalls the theory of knowledge within whose presuppositions Jaspers develops his philosophy. Hence, when Jaspers says "the judgment that is ultimately decisive for him is not even that of the men he respects, although this is the only judgment accessible in the world; only the judgment of God can be decisive,"[27] it seems as if he were affirming traditional Christian faith. But this could not be farther from the fact. The individual, says Jaspers, who in "a truly solitary heroism" seeks himself in order to conform to his own self, alone has "deep roots in authentic being, and this, stated explicitly, would be the judgment of God rather than of men."[28] The "judgment of God" as here used is not what religious faith has commonly meant by the "judgment of God." It is what a philosophical existentialist maintains is consistent with his theory of knowledge. Such "a judgment of God" is a distinction internal to an individual's own experience. From the point of view, therefore, of one who believes that there is a divine reality transcendent of human life, whose law is the ultimate authority by which men ought to live, the statement of Jaspers is thoroughgoing subjectivism.

"Authentic being" is another term which is misinterpreted when one thinks that Jaspers uses this term, for example, as St. Thomas uses it. The authentic being of which Jaspers speaks is a type of life which can be attained only when an individual is himself, and is not dependent upon authorities external to himself which define for him what he does. The "only escape from this emptiness" of living, which is conformity to authorities external to oneself, "is for man himself as an individual to win authentic being as the foundation of his decisions."[29] "The foundation," however, for authentic being is not external to, or transcendent of, an individual. It is a type of living. Such a type of living has occurred, says Jaspers, "in history when individuals staked their lives through obedience to an absolute imperative."[30] But one needs only to remember that for Jaspers the source of "an absolute imperative" is internal to the individual himself. "The unconditional is a foundation of actions," and is itself an acting. It is not an authority to be discovered by orienting one's life to a reality transcendent of one's life, such as St. Paul, or St. Augustine would maintain. "In the world the only authentic thing for man is man."[31]

Jaspers frequently uses the term "faith." This term may be construed by some to mean the act of an individual by which he puts himself into a relationship with a reality transcendent of himself. But this is not the sense of the term as used by Jaspers. Faith is an experience; and all that is ever discovered in faith, and in reflecting on faith, is an individual's own experience. "Reflection on God clarifies our faith."[32] It would be difficult to have a clearer statement. What Jaspers declares is that in our reflecting upon life, our attitude toward life itself becomes clear. Thus, our faith "confers no secure knowledge, but it gives certainty in the practice of life."[33] This means that faith is not a condition for knowing the Law of God as a transcendent reality. Faith is confidence. It is the type of life in which an individual is in control of his own resources. It is a life in which an individual depends upon himself; and what is more, trusts himself to the complete exclusion of any reality other than himself.

There is, according to Jaspers, no knowledge of God which can be communicated by institutional means. "The reality of God and the immediacy of our historical relation to God exclude any universally compelling knowledge of God."[34] What an individual can know is what he is able to discover within himself; and such discovery is of himself. When the statements of Jaspers are stripped of traditional terminology, one sees that the terminology which he borrows from religious faith has nothing in common with such faith. Able to know nothing transcendent of human experience, it is to be expected that Jaspers should maintain that "what matters is not our knowledge of God but our attitude towards God."[35] Again, if this statement is stripped of its religious language, it reduces to an explicit statement that what matters is an individual's attitude. This is what is most significant for an individual. It is to be himself. This is freedom.

Jaspers used the term "God" as Feuerbach uses it, or as anyone would use it who begins with the premise that what can be known is limited to phenomena, that is, experiences, and the organizing forms of experiences. Hence, as Jaspers points out, "To live by God does not mean to base oneself on calculable knowledge but to live as though we staked our existence on the assumption that God is."[36] The *assumption* of a reality external to experience is, of course, permissible within the limits of Jaspers' theory of knowledge. But what an individual can know is his assumption. This assumption, however, is not a clue which directs him in the process of discovering something of a reality transcendent of his experience. According to his theory of knowledge, it is impossible to know anything of a reality transcendent of experience. This means, therefore, that, whereas an assumption about a transcendent reality is as permissible as any other idea, it does not constitute a directive to designate the way in which one is to search for a knowledge of the nature of such a reality. A search for knowledge, according to Jaspers, is an operation internal to an individual's experience. "Reflection on God . . . does not bring secure knowledge, but to authentic self-hood it gives a free area for decision."[37] This means that reflection is not a way to become acquainted with the nature of a reality external to an individual's experience. Reflecting, for example, upon the Gospel is not a way to become informed of the nature of an eternal Word transcendent of human ex-

perience in whom "is life, and the life is the light of men."
What an individual can become acquainted with in his life,
according to Jaspers, is himself. Within his reflective living,
he achieves "a free area for decision."[38]

Jaspers' theory of knowledge logically determines how he
interprets even the faith of another person. He maintains that
"the purest example" of an, individual who lives by faith is
Socrates. "Living in the lucidity of his reason," says Jaspers,
"he made no concession, refused to avail himself of the opportunity for flight, and died happy, staking everything on
his faith."[39] But the faith of Socrates, it must be emphasized,
is the conviction that there is an eternal reality which can be
known by an individual who strives to know it. What Jaspers
proposes to do here, however, is to affirm what one has a
warrant to believe within the strictures of a phenomenalistic,
or even a subjectivistic, theory of knowledge.

Jaspers, or anyone else, certainly has a right to believe what
he regards as cogent; but it is presumptuous to tell another
what he believes, and to venture his presumption on the basis
of what one himself maintains is the *only* warranted theory
of knowledge. Socrates did not assume that the limits of warranted knowledge-claims are confined to phenomena. He may
have been mistaken in not understanding this, as surely Jaspers believes, since Jaspers believes that anyone is mistaken
who assumes that something of a reality existing transcendent
of experience may be known. Socrates, however, believed that
something of the nature of a reality other than an individual's
life, and external to it, may be known in his life. The faith
of Jaspers, on the other hand, is that an individual can always become more and more independent of all determinants
for his acting which are external to his own acting. In achieving this independence, an individual more and more comes
under the authority of an unconditional imperative which has

its source in his own life. This process of attaining such independence is his freedom. Such freedom is the authentic life. Thus, what sustains an individual in his life is his own freedom, or authentic being. This is living by faith, and the earnest hope of an individual is to "have the strength to live by . . . faith."[40] The goal in philosophy is "to find our way back to ourselves, and to help ourselves by inner action."[41]

The moral program proposed in the philosophy of Jaspers is to explore within one's self to find oneself. This is freedom. "Hence we must venture to be men and then do what we can to move forward to our true independence."[42] Such independence is the saving factor in life. "The inner independence that grows up in us will sustain us."[43] The direction which can be found in life is the seeking; and the seeking is the saving. What saves an individual from conforming to a conventional type of life is the striving to be himself. But in his striving there are no principles transcendent of his life which he can know, and to which it will be morally advantageous to conform. The only reality worthy to be trusted by an individual is himself—the self in an earnest searching for the self. This is the transcend*ing* reference in life: it is not an orientation of an individual to a reality transcend*ent* of himself. The attempt of an individual to become more consistent with himself is the transcendence.

There is, according to Jaspers, no principle external to an individual which can be known as a completely trustworthy guidance for him. Yet, this is just the faith of all who believe that there are principles recorded in Scripture, which are universally dependable guides for human life. According to Jaspers, however, "There is an element of helplessness in grasping at the support of reliable laws and authoritative commands."[44] Guidance is not to be found in what is known of a dependable Way, or Law, or Word of God. Guidance is to be found by one in what he does. "A man's humanity depends on how deeply he gains guidance" through "listening to the whole of reality."[45] The terminology again should not deceive. It is not what is heard—to press the figure which Jaspers employs. It is the listening. The listening is an individual's experience. If one were to speak of what is "heard" of a reality when he listens, in the sense of what he learns of a reality transcendent of himself, he would not be consistent with the presuppositions with which Jaspers himself begins his analysis of the nature of what can be known.

Jaspers uses terms which may easily be construed to have a different sense from the sense with which he uses them. He speaks of "God's help," and "God's guidance."[46] Yet, he means nothing more than a type of life itself for which an individual himself progressively struggles. This can be clearly appreciated from the explicit statement which Jaspers makes: "Once we know the limits of knowledge, we shall entrust ourselves all the more clearly to the guidance which freedom itself offers to our freedom."[47] According to Jaspers, freedom is a type of life. This type of life is the goal of an individual's striving. The striving, however, is the moral goal; and such striving is a morally saving guidance. Such striving is moral freedom. It therefore is misleading to speak of human life becoming free "if it is oriented toward God."[48]

The morally free individual, according to Jaspers, is one who "pursues only effective subjective certainty."[49] Such a quest for "effective subjective certainty" must continue so long as an individual lives if he is to be morally free and so have "authentic being." This transcending reference within life is the nature of the authentic self: "The only independence possible for us is dependence on transcendence."[50] "Only transcendence can make this questionable life good, the world beautiful, and existence itself a fulfillment."[51] Transcendence, according to Jaspers, is a reference beyond. The reference is to a quality of life, or a type of *experience-yet-to-be*. This process is freedom; and the individual who continues in this process is the authentic self.[52]

The transcending reference to a *yet-to-be* quality of life is "our relation to transcendence."[53] But the relation is internal to our experience. It is not to a reality beyond it. Hence in this transcendence "the godhead is drawn to us in its aspect of personality."[54] Thus, when Jaspers says that "we raise ourselves to the level of beings capable of speaking with this God,"[55] he does not refer to a divine reality transcend*ent* of human life. He refers to a type of life, or a quality of experience, which is freedom. This is authentic being. This much can be known. Learning this is philosophy. Hence, "To philosophize is to learn how to die or rise to godhead—or to know being qua being."[56]

After eliminating the terminology which Jaspers appropriates from religious faith, one may readily see that his philosophy is a remarkably consistent development of a system from a premise that all an individual ought to strive to discover is himself, since this is all he can know. Thus, the reality in which an individual can have a faith which sustains him in life is what he himself may be. The striving to be oneself is freedom; this is authentic being; and this is "the personal God." This is raising "ourselves to the level of beings capable of speaking with this God," which is the "way of man's self-assertion through thinking."[57]

When one reads Jaspers' philosophy as a consistent development of a theory of knowledge limited to the Kantian premise, one wonders how this beautifully written, lucid philosophy could be cited within the Christian Church as a creed of Christian faith. If there is a philosophy which is contradictory of the Christian faith that "in him was life, and the life was the light of men," it is this type of philosophical existentialism.

2. *A theory of knowledge logically determines a moral philosophy*

What one believes about the nature of knowledge sets limits to what one also believes about the nature of moral principles. Or, it may be more defensible to say that what one believes about the nature of knowledge should determine what he believes about the nature of moral principles. This qualification presupposes that one thinks consistently; and yet, it is just such thinking which is not respected in eclectic philosophies. An eclectic philosophy consists of selections from what others have said, but without any serious concern about the consistency of such selections. It is, however, just this intellectual irresponsibility which characterizes the thinking of many today, who select at random from popular existentialist philosophies, and interpret the selections in accommodation to what they assume the existentialist philosophers maintain.

Existentialist philosophers who are frequently quoted know very well what they maintain. But it is too often individuals who quote them who do not know this. Such misunderstanding is understandable. It has its basis in the diversity of senses with which some words are used. A word used in a philosophical system does not always have the same sense which it has outside the system, since the presuppositions underlying a philosophy determine the sense of words in the philosophy—provided, of course, the philosophy is internally consistent. The thought of Jaspers is one such example of an internally consistent philosophy. The thought of Gabriel Marcel is another. No charge of logical incompetency can be directed against these men, even when one does not himself agree with their basic presuppositions. Both are consistent, and both are clear about what they think; but one cannot thoroughly un-

71

derstand what they say until he understands their theory of knowledge.

The development of a consistent philosophy is always from a point of view; and the point of view defines the content of the philosophy itself. Logically consistent philosophy is an explication, or a setting forth, of a point of view. When one is clear about the point of view which constitutes the basic presuppositions of a philosopher, he then is in a position to understand the philosopher. But when he is not clear about this most elementary and philosophically most essential basis of a philosophy, he simply does not know what a philosopher maintains, even though he is literate enough to be able to read his words. It is, therefore, impossible to understand what is at stake in a moral philosophy developed within the scope of an existentialist's presuppositions until one understands the presuppositions of an existentialist philosophy. It is, however, just this failure which handicaps many today who quote the language of existentialists without understanding just what the existentialists maintain.

One who reads their philosophies cannot help but be impressed by the clarity with which they develop their philosophies; but such developments are, of course, within the scope of their own premises. What is not within the scope of their premises, however, are the senses of the words as used in non-existentialist discourse. The reason for this is obvious. Every philosopher uses words current in the language in which he writes. One of his problems is to indicate how he uses these words; and the existentialist philosophers mentioned above do exactly this. But when a reader does not take time to find out what these definitions are, and assumes that the sense of a word is always the same for everyone, there is no wonder that confusion is thrice confounded in the popular philosophizing about existentialist philosophies. Whatever one may think about the philosophies of Jaspers, Marcel, and Sartre, he cannot accuse them of logical incompetency within the scope of the presuppositions with which they themselves begin their reflections. They are perfectly aware of what they believe. It is the individual too often who quotes them as an eclectic who isn't aware of what they believe.

When Marcel speaks of a "metaphysic," for example, it is natural that another should assume that metaphysic for Marcel means, as it does in traditional philosophy, a theory of the nature of *all reality*. Although not using the term "metaphysics," Aristotle did, nevertheless, propose to interpret the nature of First Principles of all reality. But Marcel is not interested in this type of philosophy. He declares that what motivates him in his philosophical inquiries is "to know not so much what reality is, as what we mean when we assert its existence."[58] The contrast of these two points of view is clear. Marcel is concerned to ascertain what the philosopher himself means when he talks about reality. This is certainly an important philosophical problem, and it constitutes the program of Logical Empiricists. But it is not the project which Socrates, Plato, Aristotle, St. Augustine, and St. Thomas outlined for their philosophical inquiries.[59] Marcel is interested in an inquiry into the meanings of philosophical statements as manifestations of what individuals think. Plato and Aristotle, as well as St. Augustine and St. Thomas, desired to formulate a philosophy whose propositions would be informative of the nature of reality. They were concerned above all else with the enlightenment of human life by interpretations informed of the nature of all the reality of which an individual should take account in his philosophy. Marcel is also interested in enlightenment, but it is an enlightenment about a much more restricted reality. He declares that his "central metaphysical preoccupation . . . was to discover how a subject, in his actual capacity as subject, is related to a reality

73

which cannot in this context be regarded as objective, yet which is persistently required and recognized as real."[60]

The philosophy which Marcel proposes to formulate may also be interpreted as an inquiry into the nature of reality which is philosophically significant *for him*. But the reality whose nature he proposes to interpret is the subject who philosophizes.[61] Aristotle is likewise interested in the philosopher, but he believes that a philosopher is one who seeks to know the nature of the First Principles of all reality. If one is to understand Marcel's philosophy, he must recognize that Marcel and Aristotle use "metaphysic," or "Philosophy of First Principles," in very different senses. The basic principles of which each proposes to know something are different realities. For Aristotle, there is a reality other than the individual whose nature Aristotle proposes to interpret. But for Marcel, *the* significant reality is the individual who *recognizes* a reality, and who *requires* it. The "requiring" and the "recognizing" are experiences.

Marcel is perfectly aware that as stated, this would make metaphysics a species of psychology, and he therefore undertakes to distinguish metaphysics and psychology. He says that psychology "limits itself to defining attitudes without taking their bearing and concrete intention into account."[62] That there may be some such psychologies is quite possible; but they certainly would be instances of excessive abstraction. A competent psychological study of an individual's attitude is one which takes into account what the individual himself believes about the context to which he is related; and every phenomenological analysis within psychology does just this. An analysis of an individual's attitude would otherwise be purely academic unless an analyst were aware of what an individual himself believes about objects which for him are "real."

Yet, when this more defensible interpretation of psychology

is maintained, it is then clear that there is no fundamental difference between the metaphysic of which Marcel speaks, and a psychology regarded as an analysis of an individual's *attitude about the objects.* When, however, psychology is defined as Marcel defines it, it is possible to distinguish it from metaphysics, and do so without regarding metaphysics as an inquiry into the nature of a reality external to an individual. Marcel is interested in reflecting upon experience,[63] and not upon the nature of a reality external to, and so transcendent of, experience. He says, "I am convinced that I can be creative as a philosopher only for so long as my experience still contains unexploited and unchartered zones."[64] It is clear that what he is interested in is "experience." It is this which "contains unexploited and unchartered zones." Plato, Aristotle, St. Augustine, and a host of others in the philosophical tradition of the Western World, however, assume that there are "unchartered zones" of reality transcendent of an individual's life and transcendent of all human experience, which, if explored until at least partially understood, would enable an individual to be more enlightened than he would be without such knowledge. But for Marcel, "experience being like a promised land," "has to become, as it were, its own beyond."[65]

There is nothing ambiguous about this. Marcel is talking about one very definite area of exploration within which philosophy may certainly be confined. Philosophy may be constricted to any scope of inquiry. Hence, it is perfectly possible to philosophize about the "unchartered zones" of experience.[66] Yet, when this is the scope of philosophy, metaphysics must be defined, as Marcel defines it: "metaphysical knowledge consists essentially in the steps whereby experience, instead of evolving technics, turns inwards towards the realization of itself."[67] It would be difficult to conceive of any statement clearer than this.

Marcel is to be commended for reminding us that "experience" should not be taken for granted, since this attitude would "ignore its mystery;"[68] and he is to be commended for emphasizing that "what is amazing and miraculous is that there should be experience at all."[69] But even when one admits this, he may also be impressed with the mystery that there should be a reality to which an individual can open up his life in order that its nature may enter into his nature. This is also a mystery. Hence, why should mystery be so arbitrarily delimited to the self and its experiences? All that Marcel emphasizes can be acknowledged by one who is not an existentialist.[70] Yet, Marcel, and all who think as he does are satisfied to delimit the scope of philosophy, and so of metaphysics, to an analysis of the nature of the individual, to the end that the unique character of the individual's life may be more fully appreciated. This project is indeed praiseworthy. But, one may also be interested in understanding more than this. The unique feature, however, of a philosophical position such as Marcel's is an interest in experience as *the* most significant datum about which to philosophize. Marcel declares that "on the metaphysical plane experience is the decisive factor."[71]

One may have very great respect for a philosopher who stresses the need to acknowledge the individual, and to be aware of the mystery of his experience; but it is surely arbitrary to place the emphasis upon the individual and his experience as "*the* decisive factor."[72] It is *a* factor; and a very important one. Important though it is, one may also be aware of the vast range of a world existing transcendent of experience.

Philosophers' interests differ, and their interests delimit the scope of their inquiries. This is as true for Socrates as it is for Marcel. Socrates was not interested in the nature of the physical world. He explicitly states this. But his lack of interest in this inquiry certainly ought not to be construed as an indication of the scope of philosophically significant inquiry. It is simply a preference. The delimitation of an exploration to the "unchartered zones" of experience is biographically interesting; but it is not metaphysically significant. It is an expression of preference that one is interested to speculate, as did the Milesians, about the nature of the physical world; and that others, such as Socrates and modern existentialists, are interested to inquire primarily into the nature of an individual and his experiences.

The very limited scope of Marcel's interest in philosophizing becomes clear when he speaks of "metaphysical evidence,"[73] and what is metaphysically significant. He speaks of "the metaphysical problem of pride" as "an essential—if not the vital—question."[74] One may, however, regard pride as a handicap with which an individual philosophizes, and by virtue of which is prevented from becoming aware of the vast riches of life excluded from him because of his attitude; and yet, one need not be preoccupied with pride as a "metaphysical" problem. Pride is a problem. But the problem with which one is confronted in understanding the significance of pride is not to be confused with a reality from which one is excluded by virtue of his pride. What Marcel stresses is sound indeed; but what is confusing is the term "metaphysics" when he speaks exclusively about features of an individual rather than about features also of a reality to which an individual may be related.

Pride is a handicap because it constitutes a restricting, or a constricting, of an individual's life to the narrowed scope of himself. But after this is acknowledged, one still may say that knowing this much, one knows nothing more than the peculiarities with which experience itself is limited. Pride constitutes a moral problem. It is moral in so far as it prevents an individual from being responsive to, and sensitive to, a reality external to himself, whether it be other human life;

the physical world; or a divine reality transcendent of the physical world.

The significance of pride is metaphysical only if the nature of man were essentially constituted by pride. But in so far as it is a handicap which is controllable, it is a moral problem.[75]

Even after pride were diminished, or removed—and even a removal of pride from human life may well be possible—one may still be concerned to know what there is for an individual to discover and to know.

One may well be grateful to Marcel for his able emphasis upon the problem of pride as a handicap to life, without, however, following him in the thesis that it is a "metaphysical problem."[76] One might rather say that pride prevents an individual from becoming aware of the profoundly important metaphysical problems of the nature of the divine reality, and the nature of the principles by which an individual may live wisely and richly in his life when he discovers the directive significance of a reality other than human life.

Just what Marcel means when he uses the terms "metaphysic" and "ontological" becomes clear when he analyzes the nature of "fidelity." He says that "fidelity is ontological in its principle,"[77] and by this he means that fidelity makes the difference in the quality of life, and in the effect of whatever impinges upon life. "In this case, everything depends on me, and my inward attitude."[78] What depends on an individual is what he admits into his life. But the reality whose significance he admits into his life does not depend upon him for its existence. Whatever *significance* enters into an individual's life does, on the other hand, depend upon the individual for its existence *in his life*. Marcel, however, is not interested in the nature of a reality external to an individual. He is interested to understand what there is which takes place *within* an individual. This is indeed significant; but significant though the problem is, it is, nevertheless, arbitrary to maintain that this is *the* philosophically significant problem. It is only *a* philosophically significant problem. There are others, and among them is the inquiry into the nature of a reality external to an individual's life which may be known when "creative fidelity"[79] is a characteristic feature of an individual's life rather than "pride," which acts as "a principle of destruction."[80]

Marcel maintains that "fidelity is ontological in its principle" because it affects whatever takes place in an individual's life. It might, however, be said that the significance of fidelity is moral: it affects what an individual experiences in his life. Even though there is a physical world and even though there is a divine reality transcendent of it, an individual can become aware of their significance for his life only when he looks beyond himself with an eagerness to know them. Yet, even after admitting that "loving with all one's heart and all one's mind" is an essential condition for relating oneself to the divine reality, still one may be interested to think about the nature of this reality to the end of understanding in an authentic, though partial, manner the nature of what he worships. This is also an interest which may be the basic point of view of a philosophy; but this interest refers an individual beyond himself to a reality other than himself. It is this reference, however, which is not sufficiently respected by Marcel.

One may admit with Marcel that fidelity is a condition essential in life for attaining the quality of life which is most worthy to be desired, and yet, he need not maintain with him that there is an "eminent ontological value to be assigned to fidelity."[81] Fidelity is a feature of an individual, but human life is not the only reality which is philosophically significant to know. If one believes that there are realities other than human life, into relationship with which one may enter, then an interpretation of their fundamental natures may also be regarded as metaphysically significant. Marcel admits this when he declares that "a presence is a reality; it is a kind of influx; it depends upon us to be permeable to this influx . . . Creative fidelity consists in maintaining ourselves actively in a permeable state."[82] This, however, may all be admitted by one who does not limit himself to the thesis of existentialism, or a philosophy of existence.[83]

One who does not limit himself to this emphasis, or to this point of view, may be interested to know something other than an individual's life as it is affected by the relationships into which it enters. Yet, when such an interpretation is ventured, one is not an existentialist; and consequently he interprets the function of metaphysic very differently than an existentialist does.

Marcel explicitly declares that he does not use the term "metaphysic" in the sense of an interpretation of substance. He proposes an ontology without "the category of substance," which category he says he regards "with profound mistrust."[84] After saying this very explicitly, he declares that "it was in the light of this major preoccupation that I reflected upon faith and later upon fidelity."[85] His concern is not to inquire into the means for knowing anything of the nature of a reality external to himself.[86] His concern is to become aware of the affirmation he makes, and with what "takes place within an affirmation of being."[87] The emphasis is not on the reality about which an affirmation is made.[88] It is rather upon the *affirmation*. The affirmation is an individual's act. It is "an affirmation which I am."

Speaking about an affirmation is indeed something other than the affirming about which there may be subsequent discourse. This obvious distinction, however, becomes a preoccupation with Marcel. To understand fully what Marcel maintains, one must know the philosophy of F. H. Bradley which influenced him.[89] Bradley was preoccupied with the self-transcending reference of every statement, and he argued that the ultimate resolution of such self-transcending reference would be the totality of all reality, the Absolute, beyond which there could be no reference. This, of course, is a metaphysic in the traditional sense. But Marcel does not think about a metaphysic in the traditional sense when he speaks of the metaphysical significance of experience. He is, however, concerned with the distinction between the self in an act of affirming and what is said by the self about the act of affirming. He says, "by uttering it I break it, I divide it, I am on the point of betraying it."[90] There is obviously no "limit" to thinking about what one has thought, and then thinking about that thought of the thought. This, however, is a type of speculation, which having lost the good sense of philosophical health, turns in upon itself, and becomes preoccupied with itself. Hence, as Marcel declares, this is a type of thinking to which there is no limit "without falling into contradiction," because whatever has been thought, or affirmed, can in turn become an object of thought. Thus, if thinking as a creative activity is not always to be contrasted with what has been thought, the distinction between subject and object would have to be transcended. This is what Marcel refers to as "transcending the opposition between the subject who asserts the existence of being . . . and being *as asserted by that subject.*"[91]

The distinction which is made is perfectly clear. The only ground, therefore, for philosophical discussion on this matter is with the significance of such a distinction. For an individual who is impressed with the vast range of reality external to himself, and to all human life, this distinction between thinking and thought becomes rather trivial. It is, however, the very poverty of this philosophical problem itself which may well be a basis for a fundamental criticism of Marcel's emphasis. This criticism is in a sense comparable to the one which

Schelling directed against Fichte for his exclusive preoccupation with the creativity of the self; when from the point of view of Schelling, the self is only a part of a vast reality of which it would be desirable to know something, as well as something of the nature of the self.

Marcel is interested in the nature of the self to the exclusion of all other possible objects of interest.[92] Although he has a right to make such a restriction in his philosophy, another also has a right to point out how the restriction of interest to the features of the self is an arbitrary abstracting of the self from its *total* context. All thinking is a restricting of the scope for intensified attention; but the problem is just where the line should be drawn so that the selection is not to become an abstraction *needlessly* impoverished. It is this needless impoverishing of the nature of the self by abstracting it from its *total* context which everyone tries to avoid who endeavors to understand the self as it is affected in its *total* environment. But this very emphasis refers beyond the self as such; and it is in this emphasis which Marcel is not interested.[93]

Marcel declares, "what concerns us is the relation in which the witness stands to the world, what is the manner of belonging to it which is implied by his function."[94] This interest in an individual's relation, in distinction to an interest in the nature of the world to which he is related, is the basic feature of an existentialist's point of view.

Marcel is not primarily interested in a reality apart from the individual and his activities. When he speaks about an individual's testimony or "witness," he asks, "witness to what?" His answer is, "Perhaps the mistake was to conceive of testimony in a way which, by objectivising it, impoverishes and distorts it, as though it were always something of which one could make a report."[95] He certainly is right in pointing out that the individual who gives testimony is not interested merely in the testimony as an object about which "a report" may be made. But, it must be pointed out that one certainly may be interested in reflecting upon the warrant for a testimony, in the sense of the justification for a testimony. And for such an examination, one does have to take into account more than the earnestness of the individual who witnesses. Marcel, however, is interested exclusively in the "witness," or the "witnessing." The witnessing is from his point of view what is significant. Hence, he declares that "This tension between the inward commitment and the objective end seems to me existential in the highest degree."[96]

Of course, the fact of witnessing is morally significant. One of the moral monuments of ancient Greece is the witnessing of Socrates. But one may admit this, and still be interested to question the warrant, or the justification, for his witnessing. Socrates, it must be pointed out, was not concerned primarily with his witnessing. He was concerned rather with the *right* of the laws to place him as a citizen under their authority. Hence his life, from his point of view, was not of primary significance. The laws as guardians of the state were the primary concern of Socrates; and what the laws meant for him determined what he endeavored to do. His loyalty to the laws, therefore, makes no sense unless one understands his philosophy of law. It is not enough to admire his loyalty. One cannot even admire it with intelligence until one has understood what the laws meant for Socrates. But such an understanding is a comprehension of a philosophy of the status of law. Yet, a philosophy of law in this sense is not of interest to an existentialist. Thus, it is on this very point that an existentialist and a non-existentialist are as far apart as individuals can be.

Marcel speaks of the "tension between the inward commitment and the objective end" as "existential in the highest degree." The emphasis discloses his concern: it is with what takes place in the individual who is loyal. But another philosophical concern may also be in the status of the reality in relation to which an individual enters in his loyalty. These are two distinguishable areas of interest, and it is on the basis of these different areas of interest that there are different philosophies. One need not be an existentialist in order to be aware of the significance of the existentialist's emphasis. But, conversely, although one may prefer the existentialist's emphasis as the most important in understanding the nature of an individual, he need not so circumscribe the scope of his philosophizing as to ignore the fact that there is a reality other than human life, of whose nature it may also be eminently desirable to know more than we already know.

Marcel is interested in the fact that some individuals witness, or give testimony, no matter what the consequences may be in terms of hardship to themselves. This is certainly one of the uplifting facts in the entire range of human life. No one need ignore this; and yet, even though one does admit that such witnessing is one of the noblest acts in human life, still he may be concerned to direct his reflection to something other than the witnessing itself. He may well agree with Marcel that "action (is) something other than a mere content of thought."[97] Only the most extreme of rationalists would disagree. But to reject the position of an extreme rationalist is not equivalent to endorsing the position of an existentialist. There are other possible positions in philosophy, and these positions may be inclusve enough to acknowledge the sound points of an existentialist's philosophy, without ignoring the sound points of other philosophies. An existentialist, such as Marcel, is impressed by the fact that there is an individual who takes a stand in life, and makes decisions, even though such acting costs him "an official appointment and a salary on which his family could have lived."[98] There is no disputing this. One cannot know the history of the

Christian Church without knowing something of the record of martyrs. But the profound respect one may have for an individual who is loyal to a principle to which he subordinates himself certainly need not be exclusive of the philosophical concern to inquire into the status of the principle which has such a commanding significance for him. One may therefore be impressed with two things: the dedication of individuals to a principle, or a cause, and also with the nature of the principle, or cause, to which individuals subordinate themselves in loyal devotion. There is nothing exclusive whatsoever about these two objects of concern. They are made exclusive of each other, however, by the individual who maintains that only one of them is significant. This emphasis is biographically significant, but it has nothing whatsoever to do with the existence of objects in which one may be interested. Marcel is interested in the acting; the deciding; the witnessing; the giving of testimony. He declares "my concern with maintaining the primacy of action has ever expressed itself, as it has with others, in a philosophy of liberty."[99] An interest in action as the primary datum in reflecting is simply a classification of what one regards as significant. It has, however, no more philosophical significance than any preference. Preference, or selection, is not significant for understanding "existence," except when "preference," or "preferring," is defined as "existence."

Marcel is aware that an analysis of the act of witnessing is a referring to something. He says, "testimony bears on something independent from me and objectively real."[100] Specifically, "Testimony is given before a transcendence, perhaps even before transcendence itself."[101] Just what this abstraction *transcendence itself* means is a little difficult to understand,[102] since Marcel himself refers "to a certain fullness of life," although he does not refer to a reality other than such life.[103] One cannot, therefore, overstress the fact that

85

there are different interests which motivate individuals in their reflective activities. One such object of interest is in activity—deciding; giving of testimony. Another possible object of interest is the status of the reality which an individual assumes is significant in his witnessing, and which he endeavors to take into account in making his decisions. Although one may not be interested in this problem as a field for reflecting, his lack of interest, nevertheless, is not "existentially significant." It is morally significant: it constitutes a limit which the individual sets upon his understanding of, and appreciation for, reality which exists independent of his own life.

Every philosophy is an expression of a preference. Yet, in evaluating a philosophy, one raises the question whether the philosophy takes into account all that should be taken into account, and *should be taken into account* in order to be as enlightened as possible about the very problem which is interpreted.

But, entirely apart from acknowledging the preference of an existentialist for one type of "existence" as the exclusive object of his reflective concern, it is philosophically significant to understand the theory of knowledge with which the existentialist begins his reflecting. What can be known, according to an existentialist, are the features of acting, or qualities of living. Marcel declares that "fidelity is the active perpetuation of presence, the renewal of its benefits—of its virtue which consists in a mysterious incitement to create."[104] There is no disputing that this is one aspect of experience. But after this is admitted, there may very well remain the most perplexing of all moral questions; "What is the justification for an individual's loyalty?" or, "What does the individual propose to create by his loyalty and upon the condition of his loyalty?" or, "Is loyalty as such the most significant moral achievement in human life?" These are intelligible questions, but they are not raised by the existentialist. When one raises these questions he goes beyond the limited scope of an existentialist's concern.[105] Yet, unless one raises these questions, his position ends with a praise of activity.

An unqualified praise of activity as the creative feature of human life is "activism." It is a doctrine that activity is the key to the morally praiseworthy character of life. Marcel does not, however, maintain such an uncriticized activism, since he acknowledges that "The more . . . the ideas of efficiency and output assert their supreme authority, the more this attitude of reverence towards the guest, towards the wounded, towards the sick, will appear at first incomprehensible, and later absurd: and in fact, in the world around us, we know that this assertion of the absurdity of forbearance and generosity is taking very practical shapes."[106] What is disturbing, however, in Marcel's position is the very failure to formulate explicitly a criterion by which an individual's creativity and earnestness may be morally evaluated. This, however, is the philosophical problem of formulating a moral authority; and it is this philosophical responsibility which Marcel ignores because it is *not* included in the excessively restricted scope of "existence;" "being;" or "reality" which he undertakes to interpret.

A failure to formulate a criterion which may function as a moral authority is nothing new. It is the point of view of every romantic philosophy. As Professor Bobbio points out, "existentialism, even though it begins as a reaction to Romanticism . . . is unintelligible save in terms of Romantic thought . . . it harps to an excessive degree on the Romantic motif of the human personality, regarded as the centre, the original individuality."[107] The romantic preference is certainly one of the legitimate rights of an individual, but it is also an obligation of a competent philosopher to point out the consequences of such a point of view. When the creative activity of human life is regarded as most significant, the scope of a moral philosophy is also confined to activity without reference to criteria for evaluating the activity. Underlying this emphasis in existentialism is, therefore, a very obvious "distrust in face of the establishment of all possible forms of systematic and universal knowledge."[108] "This renunciation," as Professor Bobbio points out, "is based on a devaluation of morality in its law-giving capacity."[109] This tendency in an existentialist's philosophy, however, is only an implication of the existentialist's theory of knowledge.

When the scope of philosophical inquiry is confined to the nature of an individual as revealed in his activities, the status of principles as determinants of his activity is not regarded as significant. One who regards an inquiry into their status as a fundamental philosophical problem is, therefore, not an existentialist. An existentialist is one whose interest in reflecting is confined to features of experience[110] and to the individual, the significance of whose life consists in *his* experiences.[111]

Marcel's philosophy, therefore, is an attempt to analyze a type of life which may well be an alternative to the self-destructive life which is so widespread in the world; for as he points out, "we live today in a world at war with itself, and this state of world-war is being pushed so far it runs the risk of ending in something that could properly be described as world-suicide."[112] Although his characterization of the plight of the world is sound indeed, it is, however, a fundamental moral problem whether his humanistic or existentialistic proposal for man's salvation from such destruction and anarchy is equally sound, or sufficient. The belief that it is not sufficient is a basic conviction underlying this essay.

Chapter Four

FAITH AND MORAL INSIGHT

1. *The background of contemporary philosophies of existence is an era of despair*

Contemporary philosophies of existence attempt to interpret the nature of human life. Human life is always in a social setting; and it is the peculiar nature of this setting today which constitutes the specific background out of which these philosophies have developed. Marcel, for example, is oppressed with the widespread sadness in human life, brought about, he believes, by features unique to modern life.[1] One such feature is that man today has within his hands abundant facilities to live well; and yet, has no genuine well-being. One aspect of this despair of modern man, according to Marcel, "consists in the recognition of the ultimate inefficacy of all technics, joined to the inability or the refusal to change over to a new ground."[2] "For this reason . . . we seem nowadays to have entered upon," what he calls, "the very *era of despair*."[3]

Despair is a reaction of a disillusioned individual. It was once believed by some that an increase in the efficiency of man's activities would necessarily be correlated with an enhancement in the quality of his life. But increased means for efficiency in communication have, to mention only one example, in no way brought human life into a more understanding community; and increased means for rapid travel have not brought about respect for people. Devices for communication and travel have, on the other hand, increased potential military destructiveness. Every area on the earth is now within bombing distance of some military base. Thus, with vast productive resources at man's disposal, once believed to provide *sufficient* conditions for the good life, man now finds that his very life has become more and more insecure. It is this terrifying confrontation of man's life by the products of his own hands which has shaken from many modern men the last shred of optimism about the inevitability of the good life as a by-product of industry.

Having created machines to contribute to his well-being, man finds himself more and more at the mercy of machines; and his life is more and more dominated by the products which he created with a belief that they would serve him for the enrichment of his life. But finding himself *"at the mercy of his technics,"*[4] he has become aware of the fact that the achievement of well-being is not dependent upon creating equipment. The achievement of well-being is rather an operation upon life.

Directing his primary attention upon the invention of devices, however, man has neglected to train himself for the uses of his machines. Now many individuals are disillusioned not only about the worth of technological achievements, but also disillusioned about the very worth of life itself when confronted by the products of modern science and industry. "The optimism of technical progress and the philosophy of despair," as Marcel points out, are not accidentally related.[5]

The uncritically optimistic assumption that an increase in the devices for living is the *sufficient* condition for living well inevitably becomes a disillusionment. Such disillusionment is simply the moral penalty for attempting to construct life upon a falsehood. And it is a falsehood that there is a fundamental correlation between the quality of life and the equipment with which man may implement his life. There is no such correlation between what a man possesses and the quality of his life. The quality of his life is an achievement brought about by operating upon himself; not upon the equipment with which he may live comfortably and efficiently. When, however, an achievement of technics is not correlated with a moral operation upon life, the very technics themselves are misused. One need not be very astute to make this observation. Anyone who has reflectively observed must become aware of this: and it is just such reflective awareness which constitutes the basis for a new emphasis in philosophy.

The despair of modern men in possession of technological achievements surpassing anything in previous history is itself a new fact upon which some individuals reflect. Philosophies of existence express a type of reflection which has emerged in our age as a symptom of our age, and also as a diagnosis of a dominant feature of our age. A dominant feature of our age is despair; and what makes this despair philosophically significant is that it is itself a basis for a new philosophy.

A philosophy of despair arises out of a disparagement of beliefs which once were trusted. Such a repudiation of beliefs which once were regarded as sound is the hardest type of disillusionment to endure because it injures an individual's sense of his reflective competency. It is just such injured pride, however, which accounts for the emotional intensity with which disillusionment is itself defended in articulate systems of skepticism. Having trusted what turned out to be false, many refuse to trust again. "At the root of (their) despair is . . . this affirmation: 'There is nothing in the realm of reality to which I can give credit—no security, no guarantee'."[6] The tragic nature of much modern life, therefore, is that in rejecting what turned out to be a deceptive way of life, many have come to the resolute conclusion that there is *no* trustworthy way.

2. *Some modern philosophies of existence turn in upon the individual as a moral solution*

When one comes to the conclusion that no existing institution is in possession of adequate directives for human life, he either gives up all attempts to seek a trustworthy directive for life in institutions, or he looks for a trustworthy directive within his own individual resources. Having become disillusioned about the trustworthiness of institutional patterns for living, many individuals propose to seek their guidance internal to themselves. When one takes this point of view, and develops it into a philosophy, he has one type of philosophy of existence.

Such an individual does not disparage philosophizing: he disparages a particular type of philosophy. He disparages a type of philosophy which affirms that there are moral directives suitable for an individual which are already formulated in institutionally endorsed codes for living, such as the commandments in a religious scripture. With this rejection of moral directives external to oneself, the field for discovery becomes limited to oneself. An individual, therefore, is confronted with the task of looking into himself to find what he can discover about his own requirements, and about the means he himself can propose for fulfilling his requirements.

That there are many institutionally endorsed patterns for living which are without directive value almost goes without saying; and no one could do very much thinking without coming to this conclusion. But to come to this conclusion about *some* patterns which are endorsed by *some* institutions is one thing. To come to the conclusion, however, that there are *no* principles already formulated which are morally valuable for an individual's life is a very different thing. One may well reject a vast amount of institutionally endorsed principles, and yet not disparage *all* institutionally endorsed principles. The rejection of *all* directives as formulated either in conventional principles or in scriptural commandments is, however, the position which many individuals take. Rejecting all principles for living which have been formulated on the basis of centuries of individual and collective living, they propose to start from scratch. In this inquiry, they are as ambitious as Descartes, who in an attempt "to establish a firm and abiding" basis for his beliefs, undertook a "criticism of the principles on which *all* former beliefs rest."[7]

But, it must be remembered that Descartes' skepticism is a procedure. It is a method for examining beliefs; and although Descartes proposed to "doubt of everything,"[8] and "to rid (himself) of all the opinions (he) had adopted,"[9] he only reflected on commonly accepted moral and religious beliefs, but actually *rejected* none. The approach of many individuals today is very different. Many are convinced that there are *no* patterns for living stated as moral principles which are worth accepting. With this unqualified rejection of moral directives, they propose, as Descartes did, to begin from scratch. But, in their procedure, they do not readmit them, as Descartes did. Their skepticism toward such principles is not half-hearted. It is thoroughgoing: what they reject, they do not reconsider. Professor Bobbio points out that such a point of view formulated as a philosophy recognizes "no authority but its own," and it finds "itself with nothing left except to fix its gaze on man and his existence, as they appear to a disillusioned eye—cast adrift in the world, projected towards the future, straining towards a limitless transcendence and incapable of being reduced to an objective form of any kind."[10]

The proposal to explore within one's self for the only moral authority which is worthy to be respected is the unique recommendation of some philosophies of existence. Socrates has been mentioned as a philosopher of this type. But, although Socrates did reflect upon his own life, what he endeavored to discover by this procedure were principles which he assumed were innate in his mind. One may not, therefore, regard Socrates as a spokesman for the modern view of any existentialist philosophy. The similarity is only superficial. Socrates emphasized the need to explore oneself; but the self which he proposed to explore is one which he believed had a long history before this life, and is endowed with principles learned in a previous existence. It is with this Orphic presupposition that Socrates began his analysis of the nature of human life. But there is no such Orphic doctrine in contemporary philosophies of existence. Hence, there is no warrant whatsoever to point to the method of Socrates as an example of the method recommended in modern philosophies of existence for acquiring a moral authority. The method of Socrates is to *rediscover* principles for living which are already in the possession of an individual; but of which an individual is not so clearly aware as he can be after reflecting. There is, however, according to modern philosophies of existence, no such Orphic theory of innate endowments. According to the existentialists, or the philosophers of existence, whatever there is of moral significance which is to be acquired by an individual must first be *created* by him. As Professor Bobbio points out, a philosopher of existence today "sees before him existence, not as existence in general, but as the existence which is peculiar to him, as that centre of actions and reactions which is himself, and whose unique career he alone is in a position to explain and reveal."[11]

The belief that there are no universally dependable directives for human life is the very premise of modern philosophies of existence; whereas Socrates believed that there are such directives. The proposal, therefore, to explore within the self is for a modern existentialist a way to create, rather than it was for Socrates, a way to discover what is already in the self. "Distrust in the face of the establishment of all possible forms of systematic and universal knowledge," however, is, as

Professor Bobbio points out, "characteristic of existentialism."[12]

The position of an existentialist is perfectly clear: each individual must create for himself what is unique to himself. But this proposal is not only a philosophy of procedure. It is a moral philosophy: it is that an individual cannot find in *any* institution *any* guidance which is worth accepting as a directive for *his unique* life. When, however, the uniqueness of the individual is pressed to this point, the emphasis becomes a philosophical basis for an individualism which is anarchistic. An unqualified rejection of all moral directives articulated in institutionally recommended principles is not only anti-authoritarian: it is anti-authority. It is a repudiation of the very basis for a social order, since a social order is possible only when there are *some* principles which individuals respect for their directive function.

No general principle, however, can reasonably be expected to accomplish everything. To expect this, would be as senseless as to ask philosophy to bake bread. But even if philosophy can't perform kitchen duties, it may, nevertheless, have a value within the restricted range in which it does contribute significance to human life. The same may be said about institutionally endorsed directives. They are not substitutes for an individual's moral earnestness. But, individual moral efforts may be directed within institutional directives, and not in opposition to them. Yet, existentialists maintain that the moral problem for an individual is unique; and its unique character is stressed to the point of ignoring the social context in which an individual learns the very rudiments of human behavior. Moral principles, such as the Ten Commandments or the Beatitudes, are *general* directives. Yet, there is enough similarity in the specific situations for which they are directives to make it possible for individuals to be helpfully informed by their general instructions. The commandment enjoining against theft has as much relevance to a Pacific

Islander in his situation as it has to an American banker in his situation. That the situations are as different as cultures are different does not alter the fact that a principle which is morally valuable for social life, no matter where it is, does have a generality; and its generality is not incompatible with its particular applications.

It is an individual's moral responsibility to interpret a general directive for its instructive help in a particular situation of acting. A general principle may offer guidance in a particular situation, but the *realized* moral value of its instructive character depends upon the effort of an individual to interpret its significance in a specific situation.

What is praiseworthy in existentialist philosophies is an attempt to find a more suitable way to live than many people unfortunately have found. But commendable as this may be, it certainly is not the same thing as proposing that there are no ways which have been found by some that may also be helpful in one's own life. One may be most sympathetic with the zeal of an individual to find the fullest possible enrichment of life within his own resources; but respecting this zeal in no way implies that one also subscribes to the belief that the only productive exploration is within oneself, rather than within a culture in which an individual lives. From the observation that there are life-cheating patterns to which some individuals conform, it hardly follows that there are no patterns in existing social institutions which have value for an individual in working out his own moral authority. Professor Bobbio points out, however, that "decadentism expands this failure of custom into a universal dissolution of moral laws and the actual exhaustion of its efficacy."[13] He maintains that "the nullification of authority, which runs with ever-increasing momentum through the course of modern thought, and refuses in its turn to establish a new authority," is an expression of a "decadentism which has emerged in the culture of this century."[14]

One may well agree with an existentialist that each individual is, in a sense, confronted by a problem peculiar to himself: it is the problem of acquiring a directive for living which is *suitable to his own needs*. But, after admitting this much, one need not compromise his integrity to maintain that *some* substantial help for an individual may be found by learning what others have learned in the course of their living. This is not a counsel for the de-individualizing of human life. There is, in fact, no method more effective for the de-individualizing of human life than the method proposed in the romantic doctrine that an individual *creates* the content of his own life by his own creativity. Every individual, it is true, must understand his own pattern of life, and so his own moral authority; but in doing so, he may well be directed in what he learns from others, which learning is preserved in institutions.

Every moral problem is a particular perplexity in a specific situation. Thus an individual must use his intelligence as best he can to understand how he can gain specific help from a general principle. But a general principle is morally significant just because there are similarities in social situations, and also in individuals in such situations. Thus, a pattern of behavior which is morally helpful once, will be helpful again so long as situations are comparable. That they are never *theoretically identical*, however, may be argued with the same cogency as Heraclitus argued that a person cannot step into the "same" river once—to say nothing about stepping into it twice.

What is common to all morally earnest human life is the desire to acquire as much enlightened guidance as possible. What is different in all morally earnest life is the life itself which must be directed, and which therefore is in need of its own moral authority. But this authority need not be exclusive in every way of every other individual's authority.

97

3. *The nature of moral faith*

Moral faith is a conviction that something can be done to make a beneficial difference in human life, and so to increase human well-being. It is a conviction that when human life is confronted by a handicap to its welfare, man can effectively do something about it. Moral conviction, therefore, is a confidence in human resourcefulness, and in man's capacity to do something with his resources to contest the obstacles to his well-being. This confidence that man can use the resources of his life more effectively than they have already been used is the optimistic affirmation that the present is not limited to past achievement. The very effort to secure a benefit implies an acknowledgment that what already exists is less than what one recognizes it would be desirable to exist. This acknowledged disparity between what is possessed and what it would be desirable to possess is presupposed in all earnest effort.

Earnest effort in turn expresses a conviction that man himself must do something to attain a desired good. An individual with such a conviction may well be aware that there are limits to what can be done; and he may also be aware that there is relatively little that can be done in comparison with all that he might wish it were possible to do. But, if there is *any* beneficial change whatsoever that can be brought about by effort, then moral faith is not just wishful-thinking. Wishful-thinking is not a faith in what one can do to bring into existence a desired good. Existence is not controlled by wishful-thinking, or merely by desire. Desire is effective only when it is informed. Hence the intelligence with which an individual carries out his desire to achieve a beneficial good sets limits to the moral effectiveness of the desire itself. But without a desire to attain a human benefit, no intelligence, regardless of its amount, would ever be directed to beneficial ends.

The earnest decision to work for human well-being presupposes that effort can make a difference in the quality of human life; and it presupposes also the kind of existence in which changes can be brought about by an intervention of enlightened human efforts *effectively directed*. A confidence underlying morally motivated effort, therefore, is that when one intelligently works to bring about a human benefit, an attainment of the benefit is a *real* possibility.

Moral faith is the conviction that a good which *can* come into being for the benefit of human life *should* come into being; and this includes an acknowledgement that one himself has the responsibility to do all he can to bring it into being. This responsibility is imposed upon an individual by his own faith in the achievability of a good whose realization he himself acknowledges to be desirable. Such moral responsibility is the part an individual must perform to bring into being what he acknowledges to be a beneficial, and, therefore, a desirable contribution to the enrichment of human life.

If what an individual acknowledges should be done for the enrichment of human life is to be included in the scope of moral responsibility, then every individual with moral faith is confronted with a fundamental problem: it is to ascertain what *he* can do; and an attempt to know this is an attempt to become aware of one's full responsibility. Since, however, one can be responsible only for what *he himself* can do, *real* achievability constitutes the limits within which moral responsibility itself must be conceived. Hence, what *cannot* be done by an individual does not even come within the scope of *his* responsibility, and what cannot be done by anyone does not even come within the moral category. But, if there is anything which can be done for the benefit of human life, either one's own or another's, then moral responsibility includes the obligation to find out how it can be attained. Since, however, the very classification of what can be done, and what can not be done, changes with our knowledge,

99

even our attitude toward what we regard as possible knowledge becomes a matter of moral responsibility. An individual does less than he can when he does not know all that he can know, provided such possible knowledge could contribute to bringing about a genuine benefit to human life.

Thus, the very *scope* of moral responsibility itself constitutes a moral problem. The problem is to ascertain what can be known which an individual himself ought to know. This is not defining moral responsibility in terms of what an individual *believes* he ought to do. Such a definition would make moral responsibility purely subjective. Moral responsibility is not simply a matter of what an individual thinks he should do, or thinks he ought to know. It is rather what he *should do* that he can do; and what he *should know* that he has the capacity and the opportunity to know. This distinction is fundamental. It constitutes the difference between two moral philosophies.

One moral philosophy arises when it is maintained that an individual is responsible for doing only what he *believes* he should do. Another philosophy arises when it is maintained that an individual has a responsibility to find out what he should do, which includes the obligation to learn all that he could learn *if* he were to use his capacities, and were to take advantage of all of his resources for learning. If moral responsibility were to consist of nothing more than what an individual thinks he should do, it would have the status which Protagoras maintained it has. It would be whatever an individual thinks it is.

But, the very *right* of an individual to think what he does think is itself a moral problem. When an individual can be more informed than he already is, provided he were to take more complete advantage of all the opportunities within his reach to be more enlightened, his very failure to exploit such opportunities is a *moral* failure.[15] This interpretation of responsibility is not subjective. It affirms that responsibility is a matter of what *can be done* by an individual; and not what an individual *thinks he can do*. The very austerity of moral responsibility is that an individual is confronted by obligations which are other than what he himself may acknowledge.

Thus moral responsibility for knowing can be defined in a way which escapes the subjectivism of the ancient Sophists, as well as the subjectivism of the modern Existentialists. It may be defined as what one *should* know; and what should be known is not merely a matter of what an individual may think he should know. What one should know is all he can be informed of *if* he were to use the resources with which he is equipped to learn all that he might know. *Moral responsibility, therefore, may be defined as doing all that one can with whatever resources he has for making a desirable difference in the quality of human life, either his own, or another's.*

Intelligence as capacity does not necessarily make a moral difference. It does so only when it is instrumental for bringing about a change which is beneficial in human life. Intelligence as such does not constitute the nature of morality: it is only a condition for it. Apart from the instrumentality of intelligence for bringing about human benefits, intelligence is no more significant morally than any other resource which is potential for human advantage, but is not exploited for human benefit.

Thus, anyone whose life in any way is able beneficially to affect the life of another has a responsibility defined for him by virtue of the relation he has to the other. This principle applies to physicians, ministers, teachers, parents, and everyone whose life is in relation to someone else whose life is affected, or could be affected. When moral responsibility is interpreted in this way, then all opportunities to learn one's obligations come within the scope of moral responsibility. An individual, consequently, does less than he morally ought to do when he does less than he can to know what he might know, when such knowledge could be used effectively to increase the desirability of human life.

This definition of moral responsibility, however, includes the undefined terms "desirable" and "desirability." As here used, the term "desirable" refers to that which is *worth desiring*, or that which is *worthy to be desired*, when the norm of moral worth, or moral value, is the enhancement or enrichment of human life. "Desirable" is not used here in the sense of what is desired; but rather in the sense of what *ought to be desired*. Thus the definition of "desirable" itself involves the notion of moral responsibility. An individual is responsible for ascertaining what he *should desire*: not only for becoming aware of what he does desire. He is responsible for learning what he can desire that would contribute to the enhancement of the quality of his life, and what could contribute to the enrichment of others' lives. Thus, a fundamental distinction is maintained between "desirable" in the sense of *what is desired;* and "desirable" in the sense of *what could be desired,* and so *should be desired.* The *should be desired* is what can be desired that would add to the enrichment of life, and would thereby increase its value for man.

But the use of the term *value* with which to define *desirable* raises another problem. It is the problem of clarifying the sense of "value." The term "value" is used here with the sense of *that which has worth as a possible object of desire* as well as an actual object of desire. But this very definition constitutes an occasion for much annoyance in philosophical discussions. Some philosophers maintain that value is what is desired. According to this point of view, there is no responsibility to subject one's desires to scrutiny to the end that one may learn to desire what he does not at present desire. Yet, this very responsibility is implied in the definition of value as *what is worth desiring.* What is worth desiring is desirable, or valuable.

But some philosophers maintain that *what is desired* is that which has value; and it has value because it is desired. According to them, what is desired is desirable; and it is desirable in the sense that it is desired. Thus there are two fundamentally different points of view with which terms are interpreted in the definition of moral responsibility.

The Sophists maintained that what is desired is desirable; and so concluded that there is no criterion by which desires themselves may be evaluated for their moral significance. The moral significance of desires is for the Sophist just the fact that people have desires; and what they desire is desirable. This purely subjective sense of "desirable" was defended by J. S. Mill when he argued that the sense of "desirable" is derived as the sense of "visible" is derived. "Visible" is what is seen; "desirable" is what is desired. Hence, according to Mill, what is desirable can be ascertained by observation.

Mill's argument as such is trivial, but what is significant is his dogmatic assertion that there is no intelligible sense for "desirable" other than what is actually desired. It is this point of view, however, which makes a fundamental difference in moral philosophies. A moral philosophy which maintains that the only norm of evaluation is *what is valued,* and the only norm of what is worth desiring is *what is desired,* cannot even understand the point of view of a philosophy which maintains that the norm of value is what is *worth desiring,* whether or not anyone has intelligence or character enough to desire it.

The fact that there are things in life which are worth wanting, even though few individuals are enlightened enough to want them is indeed a basis for some discouragement. But there would be a basis for a *complete* discouragement if the scope of possible life were limited exclusively to the level of actual life.

There is no cynicism toward life more acute than the very

103

definition of "desirable" as *that which is desired;* and the definition of moral value as *that which is valued.* Everyone who takes this point of view already has a cynical attitude toward human life. From this point of view, there is no norm by which a present level of life can be contrasted with a level that might be attained when a more complete advantage is taken of the resources for living. Basic to this essay is a conviction that there is a difference in "desirable" defined as *what is desired* and *what ought to be desired;* and there is also a fundamental difference in the sense of "valuable" as *what is valued,* and *what should be valued.*

Defining "valuable" in terms only of what is valued is a sociologist's procedure in formulating a statistical norm. If the method of a moral philosophy, however, is not simply enumerating preferences which are affirmed, but is also passing judgment upon such preferences, then it presupposes that there is a standard by which preferences may be evaluated. A conviction that there is such a standard by which preferences may be evaluated is a faith underlying a normative moral philosophy. This implies that one function of a moral philosophy depends upon the sense with which the terms "valuable," "desirable," and "preferable" are used.

This becomes clear when one examines the moral philosophy formulated by the late Viennese Positivist, Moritz Schlick. Schlick declares that "When I recommend an action to some one as being 'good' I express the fact that I desire it."[16] In this sense, the term "good" designates what one himself regards as having value. The point of view argued here, on the other hand, is that in addition to what an individual approves or endorses at any particular time in his life, there is also the character of an *enlightened* approval or endorsement which it would be *desirable to know.* A knowledge of this would also be a moral norm, but its nature may be very different from the desires of which an individual is already aware. Schlick maintains, as the Greek Sophists maintained, that "opposing normative and factual sciences is fundamentally false," because statements about norms which are other than actual preferences cannot be verified.[17] What may be observed is what individuals prefer; value; or desire. Hence, from this point of view, moral philosophy may use the terms "preferable," "valuable," "desirable," as *preferred; valued; desired.*

This is a clearly stated position, but it differs fundamentally from the position which is here being defended. Schlick maintains that "Ethics has to do entirely with the actual," and he declares that "this seems to be the most important of the propositions which determine its task."[18] The point of view of this essay, on the other hand, is that one aspect of moral responsibility is to ascertain which goods in life should be wanted so that when desired, and also attained, one's life will itself achieve a morally worthy significance.

Moral faith, according to this view, is a conviction that an individual has a responsibility to find out what can be known about the ways in which a more abundant life can be secured for himself and for others. This faith helps to define for him his responsibility: it is to do all he can with his resources for the enrichment, enhancement, and ennoblement of life. Thus, moral responsibility includes an obligation to find out what it would be desirable for the actual to be. This is not merely understanding what one already desires. Such understanding is essential, but knowing what one desires is only a part of the task of becoming morally enlightened. Another aspect of the enlightenment of life is becoming aware of the dissatisfactions in human life which arise not only from being denied what is desired; but also from getting what is desired, and then becoming aware that after having what is desired, one's life is not "abundant." If, therefore, there is another way of acting which can be known that will be more productive of the abundant life, then it ought to be known. This *ought* defines for man a responsibility: it is to do all that he can to introduce into human life the richer content which is *more-to-be-desired* than the type of life which is already experienced. This more-to-be-desired is the normative sense of desirable.

Yet, Schlick repudiates this sense of "desirable." He says that "the question whether something is desirable for its own sake is no question at all, but merely empty words."[19] One may agree that "desirable for its own sake" is verbal; but what is not verbal is the norm *desirable for the sake of enhancing the quality of life*. If a richer quality of life is possible, moral faith affirms that one aspect of an individual's responsibility is to do all he can to ascertain what the conditions are for making such a life actual. These conditions themselves constitute a norm of what is to be desired, in the sense of what *might be desired with moral benefit*.

The notion that one has no responsibility to endeavor to find out what more can be done for the enhancement of life is sheer indolence. The belief that it is not worth the effort to find this out is pure cynicism. The formulation of a philosophy which defends this indolence and this cynicism is nihilism, one instance of which is the existentialism of Sartre.

Underlying any effort to contribute to the enrichment of human life is a faith that something can be done for the enrichment of life. Such faith, therefore, is basic for acting. In contrast to this faith is the point of view that human life cannot be altered, and therefore must be accepted as it is. When one defends this point of view, he presupposes a philosophy of reality within which he conceives his moral philosophy. Yet, when one maintains that one should accept what cannot be changed, he does not discredit moral faith. He merely states a problem. The problem is to ascertain what cannot be changed. This, however, is just the problem itself which is implied in a moral philosophy which declares that *what can be changed for the benefit of life should be changed; and what cannot be changed, should be accepted.* But, *if* anything can be changed in order to contribute to the enrichment of life, then one does less than he can when he does not make the effort to find out what can be changed. This states a problem. Hence, the very earnestness of moral faith is the acknowledgment that there is a problem: it is to know all that one can know of what can be done to contribute to the welfare of human life.

Dr. A. A. Brill, the distinguished interpreter of Freud in America, declares that he once believed it was impossible to "change a chronic catatonic into a normally behaved human being," and it has long been a matter of common consent that this syndrome which occurs in schizophrenia is a handicap which can not be altered. Dr. Brill, however, declares that he now believes that a catatonic can be restored to health, and he says that every well-trained psychiatrist "can do the same if (he has) the interest, the knowledge, and the real desire to do it."[20] This is a remarkable statement of faith. It is remarkable because it proposes a new norm for responsibility within professional psychiatry.

On the basis of clinical experiment, Dr. Brill maintains that there is empirical evidence to justify the faith that even a catatonic can be helped *if* psychiatrists are willing to undertake the tedious task. This belief that there is a way to bring help even to a catatonic is an instance of *moral faith.* Understanding how this can be accomplished is a *moral insight.*

Moral faith is a conviction that something which is beneficial for life can be accomplished. *Moral insight* is the discovery of a specific way to act upon this faith. The psychoanalytic technique which Dr. Brill used in this particular therapy is a moral insight. It is an insight in the sense that it is *seeing-into* the nature of a human handicap with sufficient understanding to enable one to become aware of what specifically can be done to bring help to a human life. Such insight is always specific: it is a concrete plan for acting. But until it is believed that such a handicap can be altered, no one would even include such specific therapy within the scope of moral responsibility; and it is only after a way to bring such help has been ascertained that there is empirical justification to confront psychiatrists with the moral responsibility to use their training to restore to health individuals who suffer from this extreme handicap.

A moral philosophy is in part a reflection upon what is regarded as worth expending effort to achieve. This means that it is confined to what is believed to be achievable. Hence, the meaning of moral worth is not defined for an individual by his moral philosophy. Rather, what he regards as worthy of his earnest effort determines what his moral philosophy will be. A moral philosophy includes an affirmation of what an individual believes is the justification for living; but one does not come to his belief about the justification for living from his philosophy. His philosophy, instead, is a statement of his conviction of what justifies living; and such a conviction, or faith, is the premise with which he begins his philosophizing. Thus, although a moral philosophy is a clarification of an individual's beliefs, it also presupposes that he has beliefs; and the beliefs with which he begins his philosophizing constitute the limits within which he formulates a systematic interpretation of moral responsibility. Such an interpretation of moral responsibility, however, rests upon an individual's faith in what can be done; and what he believes can be done sets the limits within which he defines moral responsibility. An individual's moral responsibility is *the obligation to do what he can do for the enhancement of the worth of human life, his own, as well as others'*. But what he does to carry out this acknowledged responsibility is conditioned by what he believes can be done. A moral responsibility thus cannot be stated which does not reflect a philosophy of reality.[21]

4. *The nature of moral insight*

A moral insight is a discovery of a way to act which will be beneficial to human life. This discovery is an act; and what an individual does with this discovery is another act. One may be aware of a way to enhance the quality of life, and yet do nothing to enhance it.[22] But, unless one is aware of a specific way in which to contribute to the enhancement of life, no activity can be deliberately directed for the *actual* enhancement of life.

Becoming aware of a way to achieve a desired good is an insight into the conditions which must be fulfilled for an attainment of the desired good. When a desired objective of effort is seen in the light of the conditions by which it can be accomplished, an individual makes a real discovery. A psychiatrist, for example, may wish intensely that it were within the range of his capacity to help a handicapped individual, and yet, until he discovers a way in which this can be done, his desire is not sufficient to accomplish this wished-for objective. But when he becomes aware of what he can do to bring a specific help to an individual, he then has knowledge of a specific pattern for acting. The discovery of such a pattern is an insight.[23]

Insight is seeing relations in a way which enables an individual to direct his efforts.[24] The direction of efforts by a pattern is purposive activity; but until an individual becomes aware of a pattern for acting, he cannot act *purposively*. The purpose in acting is to attain an objective; and the objective itself defines the conditions which must be taken into account for its attainment.[25] Seeing the relationship between a goal of acting and the conditions for achieving the goal is an insight.[26]

Seeing the relation, for example, between the psychoanalytic technique and the restoration to health of an extreme catatonic is an insight into the nature of catatonia in terms of a therapy; and it is an insight into the moral possibilities of a particular therapy to understand its effectiveness for bringing about human welfare. Becoming aware of newly understood possibilities for a particular therapy is an extension of the scope of its moral significance. But an actual extension of the scope of its application rests upon an insight into what can be done with a particular therapy. It is this *seeing-into* the fuller possibilities for benefiting human life which is the nature of all moral discovery.

Moral discovery is an awareness of what can be done to increase the benefits for human life, both by a reduction of *needless* handicaps to its well-being, and also by the positive enhancement of its quality. An individual who becomes aware of a way to bring about such benefits is a "moral creator." By this term, Bergson refers to an individual who sees in his "mind's eye a new social atmosphere, an environment in which life would be more worth living . . . a society such that, if men once tried it, they would refuse to go back to the old state of things."[27]

After a psychiatrist, for example, becomes aware of a real possibility to bring help to an individual, he is not satisfied with what he does until he has done what he believes can be done. But such a dissatisfaction would never occur to an individual who believes that nothing can be done to alter mental handicaps. It is only after one discovers a way to bring help to those who need it that he finds himself confronted with an obligation of which he was not even aware before his discovery. An individual's *acceptance* of his responsibility to do all that he can to make a beneficial difference in the quality of life is a moral decision; and an awareness of what specifically can be done to bring about such a desired difference is a moral insight.

In such an insight, human life is seen in relation to its possibilities. The awareness of its possibilities is a discovery. In making this discovery, an individual becomes, as it were, a "conqueror," to borrow another term from Bergson.[28] He becomes a conqueror over ignorance when he discovers a way to increase the well-being of human life. Such a moral discovery is seeing what can be done; and since a morally earnest individual is concerned to do what he can do to bring such benefit into being, his discovery defines for him his responsibility.

His responsibility is to act upon his insight in a way which will bring into existence the good he himself regards as achievable. Without understanding what can be done to attain a desired good, the good would remain an object, not of acting, but of desire. Such a conversion of *an object of desire* into *an object upon which one acts* is made possible through an insight, which is a discovery of a way to act to bring about what one desires. If, however, there were no desire to do what one can do to make a beneficial difference in the quality of life, there would be no effort expended even to find a way to act. The effort to discover a way to act which is beneficial is, therefore, a necessary condition for finding a way. But why anyone should search earnestly to find such a way is the mystery of the moral life itself.

What has been designated *insight* has also been designated *intuition*. The term "intuition" also refers to an experience in which an individual apprehends relationships between conditions for attaining an objective and the objective which he desires to attain. Schweitzer uses the term "intuition" with the same sense as "insight" is used here. He compares a moral intuition and the creative awareness of an artist who sees a specific relationship between the materials with which he works and new organizations of such materials. Becoming aware of new arrangements in the medium with which he works is artistic intuition, or artistic insight. The seeing into the nature of material at one's disposal in terms of what one can do with it to bring into existence a new form is artistic discovery. It is a discovery of the artistic significance of material; and such a discovery is an awareness of how it can be used to bring into being an artistically significant composition. It is this type of activity which also constitutes the nature of moral insight. A moral insight is a discovery of what can be done with the resources at one's disposal for introducing into life a new quality. The condition for this achievement is an awareness of the means by which the resources within an individual's control can be operated upon in a way to bring about this achievement. The insight is itself the opening up of a new possibility for acting; and when this insight occurs, an individual comes into possession of a new direction for his life.

Moral progress either in individual or collective life depends upon *influencing* behavior by principles which either are more adequate than those which have already directed practice, or else are more adequately understood than they were previously. A principle, however, which is not informed of all that ought to be taken into account does not become more informed by the mere resolve that it must effectively direct life. A principle which does not take into account all the factors with which adjustment must reckon is morally inadequate. Rethinking it does not diminish its deficiency. If its deficiency is its failure to take into account enough of the factors with which behavior must reckon in order to contribute to human well-being, then the only possibility for attaining well-being rests upon the introduction into life of a new pattern which is more informed.

Principles for life are deficient when they do not take into account all the conditions with which one must reckon to attain a type of life which is desirable, in the sense of *worthy to be desired.* But it is not enough to be aware of what is desirable. One must also know how the desirable good can be attained. The proposal of methods for attaining it is the function of moral directives; and their adequacy for directing is their moral suitability.

One persistent problem, however, in life is to ascertain whether it is principles which are deficient, or whether it is an individual's interpretation of them which is deficient. This problem is whether moral principles already formulated as directives for life are inadequate; or whether an individual's use of them is inadequate.

It is assumed by modern Existentialists that institutionally endorsed directives are inadequate for an individual's life. But all that has been said about moral insight as a discovery of new principles may also be applied to an analysis of an individual's responsibility to ascertain the significance of moral principles which are already formulated. Whenever an individual understands how he may be helpfully directed by a principle already formulated, *he* acquires a new insight into the significance of the principle. Moral insight is not only a matter of creating new principles: it is also a matter of understanding as fully as one is able principles which already are formulated.

Moral insight is an individual's awareness of *his* responsibility in a particular situation. One means for achieving this insight may be by the help of principles which already are formulated. Understanding a principle as it applies to an individual in *his* particular situation may, therefore, be as much a creative act as the formation of a new principle. A modern conviction, however, is that the only opportunity to be creative is to affirm a self without benefit of institutionally endorsed moral directives.

But an individual cannot create in a vacuum, and it is needless to begin from scratch. A rich pattern of life does not emerge from a life without content any more than significant insights in science, or in art, emerge without cultural foundations. A morally serious individual, therefore, has a unique problem and responsibility to interpret principles already formulated in an institutional context in a way which will enable him most effectively to use them for human well-being, provided, of course, they can be morally effective when understood.[29]

Moral insight is an acknowledgement of an individual's obligation in a particular situation; and the obligation he *accepts* as *his* responsibility is *his* moral authority. Every moral authority is an acknowledgement that there is a specific duty imposed upon an individual by virtue of *his* specific capacities to do what he can for human benefit in a specific situation. The specificity with which such an obligation becomes apparent to an individual is *his* moral authority.

A general principle may be reflected upon with comparative indifference to its concrete demand upon one's life; but an insight which confronts an individual with a specific responsibility is a moral authority.[30] An insight becomes an authority only when an individual's acting is influenced by it. An *accepted* obligation is acting upon conditions which are believed to be essential for attaining what is regarded as desirable, in the sense of worthy to be desired. Just what these conditions are *believed to be* depends upon the capacity of an individual to think; and for this reason, consistency of thinking is a condition for attaining a moral end. Only an individual who can think consistently is able to define for himself obligations which are consistent with the end he himself desires to attain.[31] But a moral end is not just a product of consistent thinking. What an individual believes he may attain as a beneficial good to justify his earnest effort expresses his moral insight. Since an individual's moral authority is what he believes he ought to do, an acceptance of the ought is, in one sense, his moral end.

What an individual strives to accomplish is limited to what he believes is worth accomplishing. One may not, therefore, say that an individual accomplishes what he believes is worth accomplishing. There often is a disparity between the norm which an individual respects and what he does. But, what he recognizes as worthy sets limits to what he does to meet with his own approval. It is in this sense, as Aristotle says, that "the end appears to each man in a form answering to his character."[32]

What an individual endeavors to accomplish is what he considers to be desirable, or worth desiring; and what actually is accomplished through effort is limited to that for which an individual strives. In this sense, there is a moral conditioning of achievement by character. Even the insight which challenges an individual with a future obligation is not without roots in his past. It has its roots in the very life which is less than an individual acknowledges it should be. Yet, just what an individual believes his life should be is at least in part a manifestation of what he has already succeeded in becoming.

Moral insights are cumulative. One lays a foundation for another. Any effort to conform to a norm which demands more of an individual than he has achieved to date is an indication that another even more exacting norm may later be imposed by the individual upon himself. An index of moral progress is the increasing demand of obligations to which an individual holds himself responsible. Yet, the responsibility which he acknowledges for fulfilling obligations is also an index of obligations he already has respected.

The conditioning of interests by what an individual is, however, does not imply a metaphysical determinism.[33] If interests were completely determined by previous interests, moral *responsibility for changing interests* would be repudiated. It is, of course, a fact that insistent interests do make it difficult

115

to cultivate other interests which are uncongenial to them; yet, what it is difficult to do must not be confused with what it is impossible to do.

Moral responsibility presupposes that an individual can make a difference in the quality of his life even though he is handicapped by self-imposed obstacles; and that he can redirect his life, and so can cultivate other interests. Moral insight is an awareness of what one can do that is worth doing, so that in doing it, he attains a worthiness which warrants his efforts and justifies his life. But if an individual were not convinced of the soundness of this moral faith, he would never make an effort to act upon an insight.

5. *Moral insight becomes moral authority*

An individual's *acceptance* of a responsibility as his own obligation makes the difference between a moral authority and an authoritarian demand. Acting may be coerced by socially-imposed demands; but such demands are no more a matter of moral authority than the demands of a master over a slave. A moral authority is an *accepted* responsibility to increase human well-being, one's own, or another's.

No demand which is imposed by a group can force an individual to desire either his own or another's welfare. It can at most provide penalties for those who are inconsiderate of others' welfare. But, the actual concern for human welfare is something which no social force can coerce. There is only one source from which this concern can come. It is from an individual himself. The very concern to do more for human well-being than is even demanded by a group is the desire of an individual who comes under his own moral authority in addition to the demands of the group.

The very ends for which individuals live differ as their authorities for life differ; and conversely, differences in authorities by which individuals live express themselves in differences in the types of life to which individuals give their approval. Epicurus and Kant, for example, offer such a contrast of authorities. They cannot be contrasted on the basis of discipline, because both presuppose discipline as morally essential. Many of the practical principles recommended by Epicurus as guides for living might well have been recommended by Kant also. But, there is no possibility for interchanging what Kant and Epicurus regard as the justification for living. For Epicurus, the end of man's life is his own health and his own peace of mind. For Kant, it is making oneself morally worthy by taking the welfare of others into account. Kant believes that an individual is not even worthy of his own respect unless he does consider the welfare of others.

The difference between Kant and Epicurus is as radical as it may well be, and this difference is in the authorities by which each proposes to live. Health for Kant is desirable; although it is not morally essential. An individual may be morally worthy by virtue of his respect for a principle which is universally worthy even though he is not sound in body. But this cannot be maintained in Epicurean moral philosophy, according to which, health of body and peace of mind are of *primary* importance. Kant would admit that both are desirable; but not that they are *norms* of moral desirability.

6. *Reflecting on the warrant for a moral authority is moral philosophizing*

Even the most superficial attempt to reflect would soon make one aware that if every individual were to be morally worthy by virtue of doing what he *thinks* he should do, there would be no point in discussing the problem of a moral criterion. According to Kant, no individual's moral authority is *morally worthy of respect* unless it is *suitable* to become the authority for others. This means that universality is a criterion of the worthiness of principles to become moral au-

117

thorities. But the universality of a principle is not necessarily a criterion of its moral significance for practice. The universality of an authority is only a criterion for ascertaining its *moral right* to be the pattern by which individuals propose to live.

The moral criterion which an individual's own insight proposes is morally precarious because no one can conceive a criterion which is morally more worthy than the very insight he has of what is worthy to be attained in life. It is this grave fact which constitutes the limitations of moral insight as moral authority. What an individual considers desirable as an end for which he should strive expresses what he regards as worthy of approval. And what he approves becomes his moral authority. The inescapable circularity in moral evaluations is therefore obvious: the norm by which an individual makes a moral judgment is after all *his* criterion; and although it defines for him what he ought to do, it is, nevertheless, construed according to his capacities to understand what he ought to do.

A moral problem, as well as a philosophical problem, therefore, is to ascertain the warrant for acting upon a principle which affects human life before the principle itself has been demonstrated in practice as a morally worthy principle. John Locke, for example, maintains that conforming to a principle is warranted only when there is sufficient evidence to verify the principle as a morally worthy directive. But, according to this requirement, it would not only be illogical to act upon a principle before it had been verified in practice: it might also be immoral to do so. If an empirical substantiation of the moral worthiness of a principle were an intellectual obligation even before conforming to the principle was logically warranted, the demands of logic would limit life to principles which have been patterns of practice even before men were aware of the requirements of logic. In other words, the only principles which would be warranted on the basis of Locke's argument would be patterns of actual practice. But, hesitating to commit one's life to socially untried principles on the logical ground that they are not socially verified, we continue to conform to principles which have been determinants of morally unsatisfactory practice.

It is, however, of supreme significance today whether men continue to live by an authority which has permitted the conditions for two world wars to arise, or whether they will respect another authority to direct their lives which is morally more suitable. If a principle is suitable for life, and its *suitability for life* is its nature as a moral principle, the fact that no one conforms to it offers no refutation whatsoever of its *suitability for life*. Failure to conform to a principle merely means that the principle has not been *tested* in practice. What has not been done to test a principle for its effectiveness or suitability in human life is, however, logically irrelevant to the actual adequacy of a principle for life *were it to be a determinant in practice*. But, what *constitutes the warrant* for conforming to a principle before the principle itself has been tested in actual practice is a profound and perplexing philosophical problem. When the *warrant* for some moral principles—as for example, those affirmed in the Sermon on the Mount—is not accepted as a matter of faith, individuals are embarrassed by the requirements of logic. They acknowledge the intellectual obligation to limit practice to so-called "logically sound principles;" and by this they usually mean the limitation of practice to principles to which the predominant number of men already conform. The only basis of hope today, however, is that principles which are *worthy to become the directives of human life* will become the authority by which more and more men will *learn* to live.

Chapter Five

FAITH AND MORAL DECISION

1. *Moral decision expresses a faith*

A conviction that something can be done to increase human well-being is *moral faith*. An awareness of what specifically can be done to achieve this is a *moral insight*. An attainment of well-being through morally earnest effort, therefore, depends upon a faith that there is something beneficial which can be done; upon an insight into how it can be done; and upon a *decision* to do what one believes can be done.

The test of an individual's sincerity of faith is the direction it gives to his life; and the *directing* of life by a faith in what can be done to bring about human benefit is moral decision. Acting upon one's faith is the testing of his faith; and in testing it, faith is either verified or discredited. When a faith motivates an individual to attain a genuine benefit, either for himself or for another, faith is verified, or its justification is empirically demonstrated. It is verified by the benefit which is achieved as a result of acting upon a faith in what can be achieved. Thus, in acting according to a faith in what can be accomplished for human well-being, faith is a condition for bringing well-being into existence. In this sense, faith is a factor in transforming a problematic object into an existent object.[1]

Moral achievement rests upon a faith that there is more

120

to be accomplished for human benefit than has already been accomplished; and without this faith, there would be no motivation to work for anything which has not already been accomplished. Yet, the very possibility that a good may come into existence by man's effort which is more desirable than already existing conditions rests upon the directing of one's life by a factor other than actual conditions.[2]

2. *Moral decision is acting*

Moral decision is not merely an awareness of particular circumstances for an action which is regarded as desirable. Such awareness is a condition for informed decision; but morally earnest decision is something other than informed awareness. It is *acting* to achieve an end which is preferred. Hence, it may not be characterized as "predominance of preference:" The only preference which becomes decision is one which *directs* behavior. A reflectively informed moral decision includes an evaluation; but it is *acting* to achieve what is regarded as worthy of preference. "Moral purpose," says Aristotle, "denotes something *chosen* in preference to other things."[3] It is this aspect of a morally significant decision which Abailard likewise emphasizes when he says that "nothing mars the soul except . . . *consent*."[4] This same emphasis is fundamental in Kierkegaard's philosophy: decision is the preference upon which an individual *acts,* and without *acting,* "there is no decisive result."[5] "*Acceptance* is precisely the decisive factor."

In every situation in life in which more than one action is possible, an individual has a certain latitude in acting which is a condition for *preferred acting;* and the very possibility of moral responsibility rests upon this *latitude in acting.* Without it, there would be no possibility for a moral decision. Yet, the selecting of one way of acting in preference to another is not necessarily moral decision. Acting upon a predominant preference is characteristic also of animals. Hence, acting which is conditioned by the most intense of preferences is not moral decision even if it is what an individual "really wants."[6] Moral decision is acting upon a preference which an individual recognizes he ought to want. It is therefore action influenced by a moral authority; not merely by the most intense desire, or by the strongest preference.

A decision to conform to one authority rather than to another makes the difference between a life *deliberately directed* by one pattern rather than by another. An individual's decision to conform to an authority which he believes to be worthy for his life constitutes the radical difference between morally earnest living and living which is not even within the category of morally earnest decision. Morally earnest deciding is morally earnest living: it is an individual's commitment of his life to an authority which he acknowledges ought to command his life. A decision to respect a command which one acknowledges *ought* to direct his life is not something halfway between doing and not doing. Whatever action is made is decisive; and it is the decisiveness of action which makes a commitment *unconditional*.

An individual makes a morally earnest decision when he conforms to an authority which he believes has the moral right to be preferred to other determinants of choice. Such a decision is morally crucial because it constitutes the difference between an *allegiance* to one determinant for life rather than to another. Morally earnest decision, therefore, often involves a contest of desires, in which the weakest desire or preference is acted upon. This contest between a recognized ought and an intense but disapproved desire is morally significant temptation; and a failure to conform to what an individual acknowledges as meriting his respect constitutes morally significant disunification. Such disunification is not merely between preferences; and it is not merely between ideas

122

of what should be preferred. It is a division within an individual, who, after recognizing that a commitment is worthy, nevertheless, does what he himself cannot approve.

Such failure is not always censored by an individual during an act of deciding. If it were, there would be a determinant of decision *morally more effective* than a dominant preference. Moral censorship is more often judgment in retrospect. If, however, censorship were *always* anticipated in moments in actual deciding, an individual would *always* have an advantage. But, in a situation in which an intense emotion predominates, "a reflective rehearsal in imagination" is not always morally effective.

A first step in a morally earnest decision is an acknowledgement of a way of acting which is more worthy to be approved than another way of acting. An awareness of differences, however, in types of acting is not necessarily even the beginning of *conforming* to one which an individual acknowledges as worthy of his approval. That it is even a beginning is only theoretical. It is like the priority of the potential to the actual in Platonic philosophy; or like the priority of the actual to the potential in Aristotelian philosophy. That there is first a desire to increase the welfare of human life before there is an actual decision to do so may well be argued. But the significant fact is that desire is not decision. Desire for human welfare does not bring actual welfare into being any more than beggars' wishes for princes' palaces put beggars into possession of palaces. Desire may well be a factor in decision; but morally earnest decision is *doing* what one believes will bring about human well-being.

Morally earnest decision is acting: it is not only a desire to act. The fact that there are desires which never get beyond the status of wishing is well known to everyone. Hence, it is necessary to distinguish *wishes* for human welfare from *decisions* which bring it into existence. Commitment to a specific task is, therefore, the decisive difference between wishing well for human life and working to bring its welfare into being.

That there is a *real* possibility to act upon a recognized ought is one presupposition of moral faith. But the theoretical dissection of an actual decision into what is a possibility and what is an actualized possibility is academic. It has the same arid character as the academic discussions of moral issues which left Kierkegaard so dissatisfied, and explains his vigorous reaction to intellectualism in moral philosophy. Such an academic point of view, for example, is maintained by Professor Urban when he declares that "the acknowledgment of value is already the beginning of willing it," and "the acknowledgment of degree of value is already the beginning of the choosing of the greater rather than the lesser good."[7]

A morally earnest individual is often confronted by the fact that there is a real division in his life in which he is torn between what he recognizes he ought to choose, and what he actually does choose.[8] That a recognized ought is not the authority which always influences decision need hardly be stated, since reasons for accepting a moral authority in moments of reflective clarity are obviously not the same as they are for rejecting it in situations of impulsively biased choice. A moral authority is a reflectively acknowledged obligation. Hence, it is not defined in moments when it is most needed; but in moments when the understanding of what is most needed is most clear.

A morally earnest decision is *acting* in a way which one believes is worthy. Hence, living without a demand other than the most assertive desire of the moment is a type of acting which is not even within the category of moral earnestness. A morally earnest decision is a selection informed by a concept of worth. It is acting upon a belief that what is worthy to influence acting ought to influence acting. A concept of worth is a value judgment. But a value-judgment is not a morally earnest decision. An estimate of what is valuable is an intellectual act: *acting* upon what is recognized as worthy of choice is a morally earnest decision.

A conviction about the worthiness of an act, however, is not the same as effectively influencing one's acting by such a conviction. It is a fact with which everyone is aware that a conviction which is clear when not biased by impulse loses its clarity when it is so biased. It is easy to love everyone in the abstract; but when an individual is injured by another, the principle of forgiving another often becomes impotent to influence behavior. A principle which is intellectually clear, but not morally effective, does not, however, even make a dent upon what an individual does in a situation in which impulse, and not a reflectively accepted authority, is the determinant of acting. Hence, the moral necessity to direct decisions reflectively means that an authority for life must be respected not only in moments of reflecting; it must also appeal to an individual as the most desirable way offered for his acting in moments when he actually makes his decisions.

Even an acknowledgment that a principle ought to be respected as a determinant of one's acting is not necessarily *conforming* to it as an actual determinant of acting. Aristotle compares this difference to "patients who listen attentively to their doctors, but do none of the things they are ordered to do."[9] Intellectual assent is only one element in an individual's complex nature; and what takes place within an intellectual context may have no significance whatsoever outside of it. Intellectual assent may be brought about by an intelligible argument. But the commitment of one's life to a principle to which he reflectively assents is not merely reflecting: reflecting is an intellectual evaluation. A morally earnest decision, on the other hand, is a *commitment of oneself* to a pattern of acting which one reflectively acknowledges is worthy to direct his

125

acting. It is *acting* in conformity to a respected authority. Whatever steps may take place in clarifying an authority as an intelligible guide is a contribution of reflection to morally earnest acting; but a morally earnest decision is not merely reflecting. Morally earnest *deciding is doing* what one believes it is desirable to do. It is *"choosing* what is good," says Aristotle, which makes "men of a certain character, which (they) are not by holding certain opinions."[10]

Reflecting is an essential condition for a morally motivated decision; but it is only a condition. It is not itself a decision. Although there is no morally informed decision unless there is some reflecting upon the worthiness of principles by which one ought to live, there is, nevertheless, much reflecting upon morally significant principles without any effective determining of life by any of them.

3. *Moral decision implies morally earnest intention*

Morally earnest decision is acting which is intended to bring about a benefit in human life. But an intention to benefit human life is not the only factor upon which actual moral benefit depends. An intention to enrich human life must be informed of the way by which benefits can be achieved. Abailard, however, overlooked this very elementary fact when he maintained that intention alone is morally significant. He maintained that the only factor for which an individual is morally accountable is his intention. But it must be pointed out that to act earnestly is not the only moral responsibility of an individual: his earnest intentions must be informed.

It is true, as Abailard maintains, that an action which actually brings about a benefit does not as such increase the worthiness of the intention to effect such a benefit. In this sense, therefore, it is defensible to maintain, as he does, that "when the good act is added to the good intention," the moral worthiness of neither is increased.[11] But the actual moral benefit from an earnest intention depends upon more than intention. It is this fundamental fact which may not be ignored; and thus it must be said in criticism of Abailard that the intention of an individual, for example, to sacrifice for another will not necessarily contribute to the other's welfare. An individual may sacrifice everything he has; and yet, if his sacrifice is not sufficiently informed to make it effective for another's welfare, his sacrifice as such may add nothing to the other's welfare.

Whatever benefits men have consistently achieved by effort have been consequences not only of earnest efforts; but also of enlightened efforts. Earnest as individuals have been to act worthily, limitations of intelligence have set barriers to their achievements. Thus, moral obligation is not merely acting upon what is believed to be contributory to human benefit: it is also knowing what actually will contribute to human benefit. Hence an individual is morally responsible not only for acting earnestly, but also for what he ought to know that he can know about an informed way of acting. This does not presuppose omniscience. It is humanly impossible for an individual to take into account everything which it would be advantageous to know. But, an individual has not done all that he can do until he has explored the consequences of his decisions as completely as possible within the limits of his intellectual resources. "A good cobbler," says Aristotle, "makes the best shoes with the leather that is given him." The same may be said about a morally responsible individual. An individual is morally responsible only for actions which are within his control; and he is also morally accountable only for his failure to do what he could have done that would have contributed to human benefit. Doing the best with what one has is fulfilling one's moral duty. This point of view is implied in the parable of the ten talents: an individual with one talent is responsible for using it; another with ten has responsibility to use ten. A common denominator in all instances of moral responsibility is that every individual has an obligation to use what is within his control for human welfare.

Although an intention to do what is beneficial either for oneself or for another is not affected by an actual failure to accomplish such an intended end of acting, still, the failure to accomplish an intended benefit makes a difference in moral benefits. Actual benefit to human life is the intended end of morally earnest effort; and only the intention which is actualized into such benefit is morally effective. A failure to know how to bring about such intended benefit may thus prevent a worthy intention from achieving its objective, and yet, the end of acting implied in a morally earnest effort is an actual contribution to human life. It is, therefore, a part of moral intention that benefit be more than merely intended: moral intention imposes an obligation to *do* all that is within an individual's capacity to do for human benefit. An individual's intention to do what is beneficial to someone may be as worthy as it can be, and yet, a morally earnest individual is not preoccupied with the worthiness of his intention. His concern is with the benefit which he can bring about. The worthiness of his intention is that he is concerned with a benefit to human life. Hence, it is a one-sided emphasis to maintain, as Abailard does, that it is "not the action, but the spirit of the action It is the intention, not the deed wherein the merit of praise of the doer consists."[12] Since a morally worthy intention is a resolve to increase human well-being, it is directed to an end beyond itself. It proposes, therefore, for its own evaluation not itself, but what it can accomplish.

It is, consequently, necessary to distinguish between approving a motive and approving the result of a motive. Although as Abailard says, "The external fact that the (intended) alms houses are unbuilt" does not lessen the "merit" of an intention to build them, it does certainly constitute a disappointment to an individual, who earnestly has done all he can, when he realizes that such agencies for helping are not available to people in need. A morally earnest individual is not preoccupied with his desire to benefit another: he is concerned with the other's benefit. A concern to help another is morally worthy; but it is not morally effective unless another actually is helped. Hence it is *the actual help intended* which is the criterion by which a morally earnest individual proposes to estimate the moral worth of his actions.

The actual resources at an individual's disposal, however, have nothing to do with the worthiness of his intention to use them for human benefit. The widow who gave her mite, gave all she had, and in this wholehearted giving she did all that she could. Moral worthiness is a matter of what one does that he can do. Abailard, therefore, points out that "if property had any bearing upon moral merit, or the increase of merit, the size of the purse would make a man better and worthier." It would, of course, as he says, be indefensible "to assume that wealth can confer . . . dignity on the soul, or detract from the merit of poor men."[13] Although the actual amount of physical resources an individual can use to bring about an intended end of acting makes no difference in the intention to use all of the resources he has to help another, it may certainly make a difference in what is accomplished for another's benefit. If the woman with one mite were to have had her resources increased a hundredfold, and were to have retained the same willingness to give all she had, the benefit to others might have been increased proportionately. What is intended makes a moral difference in what is accomplished; but what is actually accomplished depends upon the resources which are available for use. The norm of moral desirability, therefore, is a morally motivated individual in possession of resources suitable for contributing a maximum benefit to human life. This is the moral norm as stated in Plato's *Republic*: the resources of a community were to be under the direction of individuals whose concern is the welfare of the community. That the ideal is utopian does not detract from its moral desirability, or worthiness to be respected: the human tragedy is that resources which might be used for human benefit are so frequently used for other purposes.

The criterion by which the moral worthiness of an individual's intention must be evaluated is the well-being he actually desires. Hence intention, and not the materials with which intention operates, constitutes the basis for assessing the moral worthiness of intention. But the resources with which an individual desires to work to bring about such a desired end are not always within his control. A conception, nevertheless, of what is morally desirable may include just such resources. The desirability of possessing more than one actually does, so that more could be done, is often implied in the moral intention itself. That an individual is not able to increase the actual resources with which he fulfills his intention does not diminish the moral worthiness of his intention. It merely confronts him with the fact that he who wants to achieve a benefit for himself and for another is limited by the resources at his disposal. Such resources are not morally inconsequential for the morally serious individual. The moral idea of human life itself as conceived by a morally earnest individual is resources for benefiting human life in possession of morally motivated, and adequately informed individuals.

An individual who cannot alter the actual amount of the materials which he uses to help another, nevertheless, fulfills his moral responsibility when he uses all he has to benefit another. But from his point of view, there may be much yet to be desired. Without a desire to help another, the amount of resources within an individual's control would obviously make no *moral* difference to anyone. But when there is a desire, and an intelligence which informs desire effectively to bring about human benefits, the limitation of physical resources *does* make a moral difference. It makes a difference in the actual amount of human benefits which can be accomplished by moral intention.

Socrates made the same distinction as Abailard made between an intention to achieve a benefit and the achievement of a benefit. He also maintained that intention is the basic moral factor: an individual, he says, who trusts another "in the hope that he will be improved by his company, shows himself to be virtuous even though the object of his affection turns out to be a villain." "If he is deceived, he has committed a noble error." But, worthy as a motive may be, it is, nevertheless, a fact that no moral benefit does accrue to an individual who loves unwisely, because insufficiently informed of the actual character of the person whom he trusts. Although an individual intends to be benefited through his relation to another, his mistaken judgment, nevertheless, prevents his attainment of a benefit he intended to attain. Trusting anyone, irrespective of his worthiness to be trusted, may result in eventual disillusionment in which one trusts no one, even though there are some who may warrant it. Thus the position of Socrates that "even to fail in an honourable object is honourable"[14] must be taken with reservation. The only morally worthy element in an unsuccessful undertaking is the intention that it should be successful. Since the objective of an intention which is morally worthy is the accomplishment of the end intended, the concern of a morally serious individual is with action as well as with intention. Beneficial action is the end of moral intention. Hence, Aristotle rightly points out that although "it is debated . . . whether the will or the deed is more essential to virtue . . . it is surely clear that its perfection involves both."[15]

One may agree with Kierkegaard that "ethical enthusiasm consists in willing to the utmost limits of one's powers," and yet he need not agree that a morally earnest individual is so enthusiastic "as never to think about the accomplishment." Moral seriousness is concern for human benefit; one's own or another's. It is a contribution to human welfare which concerns a morally serious individual. Hence, the indefensibility of Kierkegaard's position becomes apparent in the statement that "as soon as the will begins to look right and left for results, the individual begins to become immoral."[16] The concern of a morally earnest individual is that there shall be results from what he does; and the moral justification for the seriousness of his efforts is in terms of the actual consequences for human welfare. The only merit of Kierkegaard's doctrine is polemical: it is a critique of the belief that a moral concern is with results regardless of motivating intention. A moral intention, however, is a concern for results; and an intention is morally worthy which directs efforts in an attempt to achieve human welfare. Moral responsibility includes an *earnest attempt* to achieve ends which are recognized as worthy of an individual's efforts. It is, therefore, indefensible to maintain that an individual's responsibilities are fulfilled by intention itself. If there are factors which prevent an achievement of intended benefits, they constitute a source of regret to a morally serious individual; but the unforeseeable and the uncontrollable ought not bulk so large in a reflection on moral responsibility that results of intention are treated as morally irrelevant.

If intentions are to make a positive difference in human well-being, "many things are needed," as Aristotle has observed.[17] An intelligence which enables an individual effectively to carry out his intention is as essential as intention itself. But although intelligence is not the sufficient factor in an action which is morally motivated, it does not follow that it is morally irrelevant. An intelligent direction of action is as essential for achieving a moral benefit as is the intention that there shall be a benefit. There would be no deliberate attempt to control available resources for human benefit without an intention that human benefit shall be achieved. Yet, the appropriate use of resources is not a matter of intention: it is a matter of intelligence. Intention must be *informed* if it is to be morally effective.

What takes place in spite of an intention is, as Aristotle points out, an "involuntary action." But even involuntary actions assume moral significance for an individual when he becomes aware of the disparity between what takes place and what he acknowledges would be desirable to take place. An individual's awareness of the ineffectiveness of his action to contribute to human well-being is not a judgment upon his intention, but upon the results of his acting, which might have been different had he done differently. The very moral ineffectiveness of acting makes ineffective acting morally significant for a morally earnest individual.

There is, therefore, a profound difference between regret and disapproval. No one criticizes himself for his failure to prevent a handicap to human life when none of the conditions for preventing it were within his control. But this does not stop him from regretting that he was so limited in his resources that he had to remain morally ineffective. When the only factor which is within an individual's control is his intention, intention is the only criterion for evaluating moral worthiness. But it is purely theoretical to conceive of earnest intention for human welfare without relation to *some* situations in which an individual can do *something*. It is the actual *something which can be done,* however, that makes acting upon intention morally earnest. An abstract intention for an abstract good is purely speculative, and not a matter for morally earnest reflection. However far such abstraction may be carried, until it becomes the abstraction of pure intention without relationship either to an individual's intelligence, or to the resources with which he must work to fulfill his intention, is itself a problem for purely abstract speculation. It has no moral significance, because it is not a consideration of actual conditions which must be confronted by an individual in making his decisions. Thus, although intention is an "essential element of virtue and character," it is, as Aristotle declares, not the *one* essential element. "The purpose of the doer," as Aristotle points out, "is a sort of measure;" but this is all that may be said for it. It is not the sole criterion of morally worthy action. No action is morally worthy without an intention to bring about human benefit. Yet, an intention becomes a condition for *real* benefit to human life only when it operates upon a real situation in which there are concrete limitations and specific resources which must be taken into account.

Character may not be interpreted only in terms of morally worthy intention. *Character is acting according to a morally worthy intention.* Actions which are not the expression of intention may be reflex, instinctive, random, coerced, but they are not morally motivated. Intention is projected action: it indicates what an individual's action may be when he *decides* to act. The decision, however, is the moral difference between intention which is proposed action and intention which is *willed* accomplishment. Will is *acting*: it is a commitment of an individual to a project he himself proposes. This is not a behavioristic definition. Behaviorism knows nothing of a self which *accepts* a responsibility stipulated for him by the moral authority which he *respects*.

4. *Morally earnest decision is morally conditioned*

Every decision which an individual makes conditions him to make similar decisions. This is a principle of habit-formation and character-formation. If an individual's acting had no basis in his character, so that it neither facilitated nor hindered subsequent action, moral seriousness would be reduced to the good fortune of making the most expeditious decision in any moment of acting. A conditioning of decisions by character-achievement, however, is the basis for moral responsibility. What an individual does helps to determine what he will be, and the decisions he makes are factors in conditioning the decisions which he may later make. It is this morally serious fact which expresses itself in the ancient doctrine of Karma; and it is vividly stated by Plato: "the life which (one) chooses shall be his destiny."[18]

This conditioning of decision by character, and the conditioning of character by decisions, however, should not be construed to be a mechanistic determinism. It is *moral determining*, or moral conditioning; and no serious reflection on moral problems would be possible without an acknowledgment of this elementary fact. "By abstaining . . . we become temperate," says Aristotle, "and it is when we have become so that we are most able to abstain."[19] This is a *moral conditioning* of decisions by character; but a moral conditioning of action is not the determinism of action by factors over which an individual has no control.

An individual's behavior is relatively predictable when conditioned by habit-formation. When, for example, an individual has acted in a particular way several times, it is probable that he may again act in like manner under similar circumstances. This predictability of behavior, however, does not come under the category of physical causation. It is a *behavior-phenomenon* that the more often a pattern of action has taken place, the more likely it is that it will recur. The number of times that physical events are related, however, has nothing whatsoever to do with increasing the probability of their causal sequence. Hence, physical causation may no more be subsumed under the category of behavior-phenomena than behavior-phenomena may be included in the category of physical causation.

The inference of moral freedom from the speculative hypothesis of physical indeterminism, on the other hand, is as unwarranted as is the inference of a determinism in behavior from the dogma of a physical determinism. The predictability of behavior has an analogical similarity to the predictability of physical events; but it is only an analogy. From an analogy, nothing whatever may be inferred: the analogy itself is an expression of a presupposition that there is a similarity. Yet, the fallacy of such analogical inference is, for example, illustrated in the moral philosophy of Spinoza. The initial presupposition of Spinoza's metaphysic is that whatever *is* determines what will be. In physical relations, this may be warranted, and the basis for mechanics is this presupposition. But from this postulate of the predictability of physical events, nothing may be inferred about the predictability of behavior. The very assumption that behavior may be predicted with complete accuracy implies the unacknowledged premise that there is *one and only one* way in which behavior can be expressed; and that is the way it has been expressed previously.

Spinoza's doctrine that "nothing lies within the scope of a thing's nature save that which follows from the necessity of the nature of its efficient cause" says nothing, however, which repudiates moral responsibility. The system of interests and habits which function in the conditioning of particular decisions constitutes one aspect of an individual's nature. To maintain, therefore, that this aspect of his nature expresses itself in decision is consistent with the presuppositions of moral faith as interpreted in this study. The conditioning of decision by character, as maintained in Spinoza's philosophy, is defensible; but what is not defensible is the inference of a determinism in behavior from the presupposition of a physical determinism. A determinism of behavior by antecedent behavior is a matter of observation; but what is not a matter of observation is that *all* behavior is completely determined by previous behavior. It is rather a dogmatic presupposition which is incompatible with a moral faith that decisions do make differences in reality, and that such differences are within an individual's control. The very possibility of morality as interpreted in this essay rests upon the difference between an absolute determinism of decision by antecedent factors, and a high probability that what has been done will have a close correlation to what will be done. This is the basis itself for moral responsibility.[20]

Moral responsibility implies committing oneself to a way of living which one acknowledges as desirable enough to warrant his efforts to achieve it. Such a commitment, however, is not a flash-in-a-pan incident: it expresses what one has thought about, and what he has made plans for. A decision which expresses moral freedom is one which takes time.[21] It is one in which an individual thinks about the appropriateness of acting before he acts; and it is upon such acting alone that a morally serious individual confers approval. Moral responsibility presupposes the capacity of an individual to control his behavior. It is, therefore, inconceivable apart from an acknowledgment of a moral conditioning of decision by character, and a conditioning of character by what an individual himself does. Moral freedom is the capacity of an individual to become responsible for what he does, and to resolve what he himself shall do when he recognizes a responsibility.

The occasion for a moral decision is a situation in which choice makes a difference in the significance of human life. An awareness that there are differences in the consequences of choice is itself a moral interpretation of choice. Only an individual who recognizes that there are real differences in the alternatives which confront him *in particular situations* is aware that choice is morally serious. It is morally serious to the extent that human life is affected one way or another by what is chosen. Moral decision is *acting*: it is *doing* one thing rather than another. It is not merely contemplating a situation in which alternatives are offered: the particular alternative which is believed to be the more likely to contribute to human benefit constitutes a moral challenge, and an *acceptance* of the challenge is a moral decision.[22]

5. *Morally earnest decision is acting to attain an end which is within one's control*

No matter how much a particular end of acting may be desired, it is not a *moral end* unless desire for it can be fulfilled, and can be fulfilled because an individual is able to control the conditions for its attainment. This does not imply that there is no moral end unless it *is* attained. It implies rather that what *cannot* be attained is *not* a moral end. The difference is fundamental. An end of acting which is conceivable is not a moral end unless it can be attained through conditions which man himself can control. Aristotle made this point very clear when he said that a moral end is not any good, but only one which can be attained.[23] He thus was aware that moral desirability must go together with attainability, otherwise an object worthy to be desired might never be more than an *object of desire*: and the most an individual could hope to accomplish even through earnest effort might be no more than sustaining his desire. But desire for an object is not morally earnest decision: morally earnest decision is *an effort to attain what is believed to be worth desiring,* and what is regarded as morally worthy to desire is also regarded as accessible through effort.

After Aristotle, however, proposed happiness as the moral end, he stipulated conditions for its attainment which repudiates it as an end of acting *attainable on moral conditions.* He maintained, for example, that "the happy man needs the goods of the body and external goods;"[24] that "the man who is very ugly in appearance or ill-born or solitary and child-less is not very likely to be happy."[25] But it must be pointed out that when factors which are not within an individual's control make a fundamental difference in happiness, it follows that happiness so defined cannot be *the* moral end; and it cannot be the moral end in so far as it is not within an individual's control *on moral conditions.* Aristotle's enumeration of conditions for happiness is rather capricious. There are, of course, a hundred and one reasons why an individual may not have children, and all of them entirely beyond his control.

So likewise, if "happiness seems to need a sort of prosperity,"[26] it follows that factors over which an individual may have no control may, nevertheless, handicap his attainment of a *moral end.* Thus Aristotle has confused accidental factors in human well-being with essential conditions for moral worthiness. No one would deny that a "happy man needs the goods of the body and external goods," and therefore, may be benefited by factors which are not within his control. But when factors *contributory* to well-being are confused with those which are *essential* to moral worthiness, and depend upon "fortune," it follows that the attainment of a worthy moral end is often impossible for non-moral reasons.

Aristotle, however, admits that happiness does not presuppose great prosperity. He admits that "we can do noble acts without ruling earth and sea." Yet, after acknowledging that "noble acts" do not necessarily depend upon external goods, he says that "it is impossible, or not easy, to do noble acts without the proper equipment."[27] Although there obviously is ambiguity in just what is meant by "external goods" and "prosperity," the fact nevertheless remains that in so far as an attainment of the most desirable end in life "seems to need a sort of prosperity," it is not within an individual's control on specifically moral conditions.

When Aristotle maintains that "the man who is to be happy will . . . need virtuous friends," he again states a condition which may not be within an individual's control *on moral conditions.* An individual, for example, who is unjustly ostracized from a society is thereby cut off from the moral end in so far as he is involuntarily denied association with others. But, everyone knows that there is a vast amount of moral heroism in individuals who have been driven from their communities; excommunicated from their religious institutions; and despised by their own families. It is, therefore, one thing to maintain that an individual's happiness *is affected* by the people with whom he associates: it is quite another thing to maintain that the supremely worthy end *depends* upon such associations. That the quality of an individual's life is affected by many factors, no sensible person would deny; but that factors external to an individual's control should make it impossible, or unlikely, to attain the most worthy end for which he can strive is a repudiation of the very justification for moral earnestness itself.

Whatever is *worthy to be an end of earnest striving* must be within an individual's control, so that by *his* efforts he can attain it. If an attainment of what is most worthy in life were to be made impossible because it depends upon factors over which an individual has no control, the most worthy good in life would not even be a moral end for some individuals. Happiness as Aristotle interprets it, therefore, cannot be a universally worthy moral end. Whatever a moral end may be, its attainment must be correlated with a *worthiness* to attain it. Nothing could be more intolerable to moral seriousness itself than the cynical doctrine that there is no correlation between living worthily and the actual achievement of a worthy end in life. It is, however, this element of accident in Aristotle's interpretation of the moral end which makes his position fundamentally cynical; and it is this very aspect of his doctrine which motivated the Stoics to reinterpret the moral end. They maintained that if happiness is the moral end, it can not be contingent upon accidents. They were thus clearly aware that a moral end must be realizable upon moral conditions: that is, it must be dependent upon what an individual can do to make himself worthy to attain it.

A moral end is a good to which an individual may direct himself with a warranted assurance that when he is *morally entitled to attain it,* he will attain it. But when there is no basis for such assurance, there likewise is no *moral warrant* to take life itself seriously. There must always be the cynical reservation that in spite of what one does to make himself worthy to attain a supremely worthy moral end, he may be defeated by sheer accident, or denied it by the caprice of factors before which moral worthiness is irrelevant. Yet, the very assumption that there is such an existence in which an individual's moral worthiness can be dismissed as morally irrelevant is intolerable. The faith of a morally serious individual is that existence is not of the type which makes it necessary to acknowledge accident as the *final* determinant in human life. *Morally earnest faith is that there are moral conditions for the achievement of moral ends.*

In some respects even Epicurus had a clearer understanding of the nature of a moral end than did Aristotle, for he maintained that "independence of outward things (is) a great good." Hence when he declared that "we are to be contented with little if we have not much, being honestly persuaded that they have the sweetest enjoyment of luxury who stand least in need of it," he was aware of the problem of attaining a moral end upon conditions within an individual's control. He was aware that an end of desire worthy of serious effort may be attained by virtue of what one does; and that what one does has real correlation with what he attains. This sound moral insight of Epicurus was developed with incredible consistency by the Stoics: Marcus Aurelius, for example, declared that men "may impede my action, but they are no impediment to my disposition."[28] He thus hit upon an essential condition for the attainment of a moral end *by moral means*. What takes place external to an individual may be beyond his control; as Aurelius says; "the world may cry against thee." But even then he maintains, "it is in thy power to live free from all compulsion."[29]

That Aurelius over-stated the ordinary individual's capacity to surmount the adverse impacts of life, no one would deny. What, however, is significant in this statement is the clarity with which he recognized that *if* there is a moral end, it must be within an individual's control. The Stoics' proposal of what an individual ought to do may well tax an ordinary imagination to the breaking point. Yet, the fact is that they did not cite the ordinary man as the norm of moral worthiness. The Stoic proposal is austere: "if any man by using force stands in thy way . . . employ the hindrance towards the exercise of some other virtue."[30] But what is significant about this recommendation is the clarity with which Aurelius thought through the implications of a moral end.

Many things are not within an individual's control. No Stoic ever believed that an individual can effectively deter all events adverse to his well-being. But the Stoics did believe that there are *some things* which *always* are within an individual's control: "a good disposition is invincible, if it be genuine, and not an affected smile and acting a part." The implication of this doctrine is that even cruelty cannot deflect a morally resolute individual from reacting to it without hate and vindictiveness: "for," asks Aurelius, "what will the most violent man do to thee if thou continuest to be of a kind disposition towards him."[31] This doctrine may well seem beyond credibility. And yet, it is the very seriousness of the Stoic to face the nature of human life which makes him maintain that *if* there is an end which really is within an individual's control, it must remain within his control even when there are adversities. Quite apart from what anyone may think of the Stoic proposal, the fact remains that no Greek philosophy before Stoicism ever grasped the full problem of the difficulty of defining a *universally worthy* moral end. Stoic moral philosophy is stern. But so are some aspects of human life. And the relatively few individuals who have thought through the problem of an end in life which can justify life itself, notwithstanding every adversity and obstacle, have arrived at a point of view which is not very far from the uncompromising position of the Stoic.[32]

Aristotle maintains that a moral end which is desired more than anything else would be chosen "always for itself and never for the sake of something else."[33] That this particular moral end should be an individual's own happiness is the peculiar preference of eudaemonism. But to regard an individual's own happiness as the good which fulfills the characterization of the morally worthy, most desirable end in life is simply a definition. It is, therefore, indefensible to maintain, as Aristotle does, that "everything we choose we choose for the sake of something else—except happiness."[34] This proposition disregards the fact that there are individuals who live for ends other than their own happiness. It would, however, be defensible to maintain that an individual who has oriented his life to objects *worthy to be desired* is *worthy of happiness*. Thus, there is a very great difference in the position that an individual's happiness is the one end morally worthy of his effort, and in the position that when an individual strives for a morally worthy end he is morally worthy to attain happiness. These two doctrines have nothing in common except words; since they differ in the basic propositions which affirm the nature of the moral end.

Notwithstanding the many deficiencies of the relatively

143

superficial moral philosophy of Epicurus, his philosophy has the merit that it is not ambiguous. When he declares that "we must exercise ourselves in the things which bring happiness, since, if that be present, we have everything," he affirms that the one supremely desirable good in life is an individual's own happiness. The directness of the Epicurean position enables one to understand exactly what is at stake in making an individual's own happiness the one thing which is of supreme concern in his life. Philebus likewise is an example of equally direct thinking: he explicitly declares that "pleasure is the true end of all living beings, at which all *ought* to aim, and is the chief good of all."[35] Thus Philebus identifies pleasure with the moral end, and so maintains that whatever is worth desiring has worth by virtue of its capacity to produce pleasure *for the individual himself*. This is outright hedonism. If hedonism is a morally deficient point of view, a clearly stated hedonism is at least a contribution to clear thinking. When one knows exactly what is maintained, because discussion is not encumbered with ambiguity, he then can evaluate its soundness as a moral philosophy, and can assess its value in terms of clarifying a fundamental problem in life. It is the very clarity with which Philebus maintains the "pleasant" is the "good," and morally worthy good is pleasant, that makes it possible for Socrates to point out the fallacies in this point of view.

Eudoxus likewise states explicitly that pleasure is the moral end. He infers that because all men desire pleasure, it is the one supremely desirable good, and as "the most desirable, is most good." He may well be criticized for glossing over the difference between desirable as a character of an object which warrants desire for it, and desirable as an attributed characteristic which is a product of desiring. But apart from failing to make this distinction, Eudoxus knows exactly what he believes. He believes that an individual's pleasure is the

144

one thing for which an individual *should* strive; and he declares that each individual's pleasure is the end for which he has a right *always* to strive. From the fact that individuals desire their pleasure, he proposes the comfortable moral norm that what they desire is what they *should* desire: "the fact of all things being drawn to the same object (pleasure) is an indication that that object is the best for all." The light-weight character of Eudoxus' value theory may disturb some people, but it does have the merit that it states explicitly what many believe.

Epicurus likewise has the merit to state very clearly what he believes to be the norm of human values: it is that from which an individual can derive pleasure *for himself*. "Pleasure is our first and native good." The very fact that pleasures sometimes are avoided, however, does not imply that pleasure is subordinated to another end. It implies rather that an individual has sense enough to know that in order to get one pleasure it is necessary at times to relinquish another: "for that reason we do not choose every pleasure whatsoever, but of times pass over many pleasures." The justification for relinquishing pleasure, however, according to Epicurus, is to enjoy another pleasure. There is nothing contradictory in this, since an individual who wants his own pleasure more than anything else in life must also acknowledge that some of his pleasures should not be allowed to interfere in his enjoyment of other pleasures. The consistency of this hedonistic point of view is made apparent when Epicurus says that "of times we consider pains superior to pleasures, when submission to the pains for a long time brings us as a consequence a greater pleasure." This is the forthright statement of Epicureanism, or of philosophically consistent hedonism: "While all pleasure is good, not all pleasure is choice worthy." Moral obligation, therefore, according to Epicurean hedonism, is no more taxing than to use intelligence cleverly enough to avoid forfeiting pleasure for one's self. The authority for life, according to such a hedonism, is to do everything one can to select experiences which are contributory to the pleasure-content of his own life. The conclusion of such calculation, with no other norm for evaluating moral worthiness than an individual's own pleasurable experiences, is that some pleasurable experiences *ought* to be preferred to others. The meaning of the moral ought thus becomes construed in terms of what an individual should do for himself.

But controlling experiences to the end that one may enjoy pleasurable experiences is not to pursue *pleasure* as the supreme concern of life. Pleasure cannot be experienced apart from conditions upon which it depends. This implies that there are certain factors in experience which must be taken into account if an individual is even to enjoy a consistently pleasurable experience. Pleasure as a moral end is an abstraction. There is no *pleasure* as an end of effort: there are, however, *pleasurable activities*. To conceive a pleasure as an end of effort is, therefore, to abstract an emotional tone of experiences from experiences. "Pleasure" cannot be attained as a controlled good without taking into account a particular type of experience which is pleasant for an individual. Yet, in order to enjoy pleasurable experience, an individual must control the conditions of experience which make experience pleasurable. Thus the notion that the *one* concern of life is "pleasure" is a fiction; it is not a moral end. Only an attainable good is a moral end.

Happiness abstracted from complex conditions, likewise, is not the moral end; and for the same reason that pleasure is not. "Happiness," as Aristotle points out, "is an activity" or a quality of life."[36] But "to identify the end with certain actions and activities"[37] is to make the norm of moral value everything which contributes to the effective attainment of such actions or activities. "Happiness," as Aristotle says, "lies in living."[38] This sound insight is that happiness, no more than pleasure, may be treated as a specific end for which an individual can directly strive.[39]

Even if such an individual were able to control all of the conditions necessary for fulfilling his desires, and were discriminating enough to fulfill only those desires whose satisfactions could be assimilated without discord into an integrated life, he would, if he were morally earnest, still be confronted with the concern for the worthiness of his *life*. Hence, if it were possible to have every particular desire satisfied, and even to enjoy satisfactions which are mutually consistent, the moral problem would not be entirely resolved. An individual would have to pass judgment upon himself, and not only upon his particular experiences. This is the profound insight of Plato when he points out that even after an individual fulfills desires, he does not necessarily experience satisfactions which he can *approve*. Yet, the failure to approve reveals the fundamental division between what an individual *experiences* and what he regards as *worthy to be experienced*. It is this disparity between what an individual has made an effort to enjoy and what he acknowledges as *worthy of his effort* which leaves an individual in the strange dilemma of getting what he desires, and yet not having what he approves.

Yet, there is no real paradox in this. It is a common fact that when an individual has satisfied a desire, and subsequently evaluates its worthiness, the satisfaction itself may have lost all value for him. This re-evaluation of satisfaction is a fact with which every matured individual is aware. It is, furthermore, a fact that an individual must *accept* his satisfactions no matter how erroneous his estimate of their value may once have been. Yet, an inability to approve one's own experiences disrupts the unity of one's life, and such disunification is not only *a* dissatisfaction—it is a dissatisfied person. Only the most superficial of theories, therefore, can maintain that the moral end is a summation of satisfactions in such quantity that pleasures outweigh dissatisfactions. An approval or disapproval of one's own life has no correlation whatsoever with the number of satisfactions an individual may experience. An individual's inability to *accept* what he has experienced as worthy of himself totally impairs his well-being. It is this fact which Plato emphasizes when he points out that an individual who does not have "the approval of the whole soul"[40] has failed to fulfill *an essential* moral condition.

If it were possible to slough off experiences as one dusts off his coat, there would be no morally meaningful heartaches, because a mistaken choice would not be morally serious. It would constitute nothing more than a momentary error, and its handicap would amount to nothing more than a temporary dissatisfaction. But to gloss over the fact that there are events in human life which some would give a right arm to have escaped is to disregard one of the stern realities of human life itself. Aristotle, therefore, does not invent a fiction when he says that an individual may be "pained because he was pleased, and he could have wished that these things had not been pleasant to him."[41] Repentance is a fact in human life. To dismiss it as a pathological discomfort is to do violence to the very experience of disapproval of which an individual becomes aware when he acknowledges that what he has done must be judged by what he recognizes he ought to have done. Hence the notion that there is nothing more urgent in an individual's life than to get what he wants when he wants it, is infantile. After an individual gets what he wants, he often has the tragic fact to confront him that he was mistaken in supposing that what he wanted was worthy to be wanted.

6. *Religious faith acknowledges an ultimate norm for the moral worthiness of decisions*

A desire to have the benefit of a dependable norm of what

is worthy to approve is a requirement of morally earnest life. The faith that there is a completely dependable reality—the Law, the Will, the Word, the Way—transcendent of human life which fulfills this requirement is religious faith. A desire for a trustworthy norm is not uniquely religious; but moral. What is religious is the faith that there is a reality to which man may turn for the fulfillment of this desire, and may do so with warranted confidence because this reality is worthy of his unqualified trust. Its trustworthiness is its nature. Man's need for a trustworthy guide is man's requirement. In his need, religious faith thus proposes a morally significant solution.

Religious faith is a proposal of a way for an individual to cope with a profound moral problem.[42] It affirms that there is a reality to which he may turn which can help him as no other reality can. It affirms that there is a reality transcendent of human life which may be known; and when known will inform his life with a trustworthy norm. Thus, according to religious faith, the most urgent moral need is, in the words of St. Augustine, to know "the unchangeable and eternal truth, so that . . . by being subject to it and obeying it we may do rightly;"[43] since this is the one "Wisdom which needing no light enlightens the minds that need it."[44]

REFERENCES IN CHAPTER I

1—*Ethica Nicomachea*, I, 1095b, 7. Trans. W. D. Ross, Oxford, 1925.
2—*Ibid.*, I, 1094a, 23-25.
3—*Republic*, VI, 508. Trans. B. Jowett, III ed., Oxford, 1931.
4—*Ibid.*, VI, 500.
5—*Ibid.*, VI, 505.
6—*Ibid.*, VII, 534.
7—*Ibid.*, VI, 484.
8—*Ibid.*, VI, 507.
9—*Ibid.*, VII, 519.
10—*Ibid.*, VI, 511.
11—*Ibid.*, VI, 500.
12—*Ibid.*, VI, 490.
13—*Ibid.*, VII, 517.
14—*The Philosophy of Plato*, p. 48, Scribners, N. Y., 1939.
15—*Ethica Nicomachea*, I, 1096b, 20.
16—*Ibid.*, II, 1103b, 30.
17—*Ibid.*, VI, 1144b, 25.
18—*Ibid.*, VI, 1144b, 24.
19—*Ibid.*, VI, 1144b, 25.
20—*Ibid.*, VII, 1147b, 5.
21—*Civilization and Ethics*, p. 44, Adam and Charles Black, London, 1946.
22—*Ethica Nicomachea*, II, 1108a, 15.
23—*Ibid.*, II, 1109b, 20. (italics mine).
24—*Ibid.*, II, 1109a, 20.
25—*Ibid.*, II, 1106b, 25-35.
26—*Ibid.*, VI, 1138b, 15-20.
27—*Ibid.*, II, 1106b, 5.
28—*Ibid.*, III, 1115b, 15-20.
29—*Ibid.*, IV, 1120a, 20.
30—*Ibid.*, V, 1131b, 15.
31—*Ibid.*, IV, 1126b, 5-10.

32—*Ibid.*, II, 1109a, 25.

33—*Ibid.*, II, 1107a, 10.

34—*Ibid.*, X, 9, 1179b, 25-30.

35—*Ibid.*, III, 5, 1114a, 13.

36—*Ibid.*, III, 12, 1119a, 34.

37—*Ibid.*, V, 9, 1136b, 5-10.

38—*The World and the Individual*, p. 359, Macmillan, 1923. Professor Royce maintains that "all sin is a free choosing of the sort of narrowness;" and "sin depends upon a narrowing of consciousness, so that a present ignorance of what one ought to know occurs."

39—*Some Suggestions in Ethics*, p. 110, Macmillan, London, 1918.

40—*General Theory of Value*, p. 584, Longmans, N. Y., 1926.

41—Professor Perry says that "over and above the error to which mortal mind is proverbially liable, but which experience reduces and corrects, there is a pathological error which is due to an unwillingness to face the facts." (*Op. cit.*, p. 585.)

42—It is in this way that Spinoza accounts for biased judgments: "When a man is a prey to his emotions," he says, "he is not his own master." This is certainly true. But the issue is not whether there is a handicap to man's reasoning. It is whether reasoning itself can be an obstacle to man's well being. Spinoza does not even qualify his rationalism when he acknowledges that man "is often compelled, while seeing that which is better for him, to follow that which is worse." The explanation he offers for this is not a deficiency in the moral trustworthiness of reasoning. It is rather an obstacle to reasoning; and therefore, a factor other than reasoning.

REFERENCES IN CHAPTER II

1—*Laches*, 184e, Loeb Classical Library.
2—*Ibid.*, 190c.
3—*Ibid.*, 194d.
4—*Ibid.*, 201a.
5—*Charmides*, 173c, Loeb Classical Library.
6—*Ibid.*, 175a.
7—*Republic*, I, 343, Trans. B. Jowett.
8—*Ibid.*, I, 344.
9—"Protagoras said . . . that man is the measure of all things—that things are to me such as they seem to me, and to you such as they seem to you." (*Cratylus*, 386a, Loeb Classical Library). And again, "Protagoras . . . says somewhere that man is the measure of all things, of the existence of the things that are and the non-existence of the things that are not." (*Theaetetus*, 152a, Loeb Classical Library.)
10—"Atoms move at random in the void and collide with each other by chance." (Dionysius from Eus. P. E. XIV, 23, 2, 3, quoted from *Selections from Early Greek Philosophy*, Nahm, M., Crofts, N. Y., 1940.) "The atoms . . . collide with each other, and all things . . . move by necessity." (Diogenes of Oinoanda, Fr. 80-81, col. 3, 3, quoted from Nahm, M., *op. cit.*, p. 174.)
11—*Lives and Opinions of Eminent Philosophers*, ix, 39, Trans. R. D. Hicks, Loeb Classical Library.
12—*Adversus Mathematicos*, VII, 265, quoted from Nahm, M., *op. cit.*, p. 217. Diogenes Laertius also declares: "In my *Pammetros*, I have a piece on him as follows: Pray who was so wise, who wrought so vast a work as the *omniscient* Democritus achieved." (*Op. cit.*, ix, 43.)
13—*Ethica Nicomachea*, X, 1172a, 10-15.
14—In interpreting the point of view of Thomas Hobbes, a philosophical materialist, Professors Thilly and Wood point out that "Sensations are not qualities of things themselves; they are but motions in us . . . All sense is fancy, but the cause is a real body. There is no similarity between the cause of the sensation and the sensation . . . If this is true,

how do we know what is the nature of the world? Hobbes does not answer this problem, for it did not disturb him; he dogmatically assumes with the scientists of his day that the world is a corporeal world in motion." (*History of Philosophy*, p. 295, Holt, N. Y., 1951.)

15—*Physics, Aristotle*, 4, 203a, 33.

16—*Ibid.*, Z, 13, 1039a, 9.

17—Galen *de elem.* sec. Hippolyti philosophumena, I, 2., quoted from Nahm, M., *op. cit.*, p. 173.

18—*Op. cit.*, ix, 45.

19—*Op. cit.*, quoted from Nahm, M. *op. cit.*, p. 217.

20—Nahm, M. *op. cit.*, p. 171.

REFERENCES TO CHAPTER III

1—*Way to Wisdom*, p. 177. Trans., R. Manheim, Gollancz, London, 1951. (Yale University Press, New Haven.)
2—*Ibid.*, p. 177.
3—*Ibid.*, p. 177.
4—*Ibid.*, p. 78.
5—*Ibid.*, p. 79.
6—*Ibid.*, p. 29.
7—*Ibid.*, p. 179.
8—*Confessions of St. Augustine*, Bk. VII.
9—*Op. cit.*, p. 168.
10—*Ibid.*, p. 56.
11—*Ibid.*, p. 57.
12—*Ibid.*, p. 56.
13—*Ibid.*, p. 56. (Italics mine.)
14—*Ibid.*, p. 56.
15—*Ibid.*, p. 56.
16—*Ibid.*, p. 56.
17—*Ibid.*, p. 55.
18—*Ibid.*, p. 64.
19—*Ibid.*, p. 64.
20—*Ibid.*, p. 45.
21—*Ibid.*, p. 68.
22—*Ibid.*, p. 68.
23—*Ibid.*, p. 45.
24—*Ibid.*, p. 163.
25—*Ibid.*, p. 90.
26—I, 12-14.
27—*Op. cit.*, p. 68.
28—*Ibid.*, p. 69.
29—*Ibid.*, p. 53.

30—*Ibid.,* p. 53.

31—*The Perennial Scope of Philosophy,* p. 143, The Philosophical Library, N. Y., 1950.

32—*Way to Wisdom,* p. 50.

33—*Ibid.,* p. 51.

34—*Ibid.,* p. 47.

35—*Ibid.,* p. 47.

36—*Ibid.,* p. 50.

37—*Ibid.,* p. 51.

38—*Ibid.,* p. 51.

39—*Ibid.,* p. 53.

40—*Ibid.,* p. 40.

41—*Ibid.,* p. 121.

42—*Ibid.,* p. 119.

43—*Ibid.,* p. 119.

44—*Ibid.,* p. 73.

45—*Ibid.,* p. 73.

46—"Often God's help is narrowed to a finite content and thus lost. As for example when prayer . . . becomes an invocation of this God for practical ends." (*Ibid.,* p. 72.) And again, "God's guidance cannot be made into a possession." (*Ibid.,* p. 70.)

47—*Ibid.,* p. 66.

48—*Ibid.,* p. 66.

49—*The Perennial Scope of Philosophy,* p. 78.

50—*Way to Wisdom,* p. 118.

51—*Ibid.,* p. 126.

52—"Philosophy is the act of becoming conscious of genuine being— or is the thinking of a faith in man that must be infinitely elucidated— or is the way of man's self-assertion through thinking." (*Ibid.,* p. 163.)

53—*Ibid.,* p. 71.

54—*Ibid.,* p. 71.

55—*Ibid.,* p. 71.

56—*Ibid.,* p. 162.

57—*Ibid.,* p. 71; 162.

58—*The Philosophy of Existence,* p. 80. Trans. Manya Harari, Philosophical Library, N. Y., 1949.

59—Professor Jean Wahl points out that "we must contrast the philosophy of existence to the classical conceptions of philosophy to be found in, say, Plato, Spinoza, and Hegel." *A Short History of Existentialism,* p. 2, Trans. F. Williams and S. Maron, Philosophical Library, N. Y., 1949.

60—*Op. cit.,* p. 95.

61—Hence Marcel regards "the problem of the vocation (as) essentially a *metaphysical* one." (*Mystery of Being: Reflection and Mystery,* vol. 1, p. 44, Trans. G. S. Frazer, Regnery, Chicago, 1949.) He likewise believes that "the family relationship is not one which up to the present has sufficiently engaged the attention of *metaphysics.*" (*Ibid.,* p. 196. *Italics mine.*)

62—*The Philosophy of Existence,* p. 95.

63—Marcel says, "our point of reference can be based only upon experience itself, treated as a massive presence which is to be the basis of all our affirmation." *The Mystery of Being: Faith and Reality,* vol. II, Trans. René Hague, Regnery, Chicago, 1951.

64—*The Philosophy of Existence,* p. 96.

65—*Ibid.,* p. 96.

66—*Ibid.,* p. 96.

67—*Ibid.,* p. 96.

68—He stresses an important point when he says that "We tend, without realizing it, to form far too restrictive an idea of experience." (*The Mystery of Being,* vol. I, p. 47.)

69—*The Philosophy of Existence,* p. 96.

70—It is difficult to know to whom this classification refers. Wahl declares that "Heidegger has opposed what he terms 'existentialism,' and Jaspers has asserted that 'existentialism' is the death of the philosophy of existence! So that it seems only right to restrict our application of the term 'existentialism' to those who willingly accept it, to those whom we might call The Philosophical School of Paris, i.e., Sartre, Simone de Beauvoir, Merleau-Ponty." (*Op. cit.,* p. 2.)

71—*Ibid.,* p. 89.

72—Marcel asserts, "I am talking merely about myself, in so far as I make a judgment that something or other exists . . . this centrally significant existence . . . is simply, of course, myself, in so far as I feel sure that I exist." (*Op. cit.,* vol. I, p. 88.)

73—*The Philosophy of Existence,* p. 76.

74—*Ibid.,* p. 19.

75—Marcel also states this when he says "An experience can be saturated with prejudices but this means that the prejudice which obstructs it at the same time prevents it from being fully an experience." "They are like distorting spectacles through which we look at everything that is presented to us." (*The Mystery of Being,* vol. I, p. 56.)

76—"Pride . . . consists in drawing one's strength solely from oneself.

The proud man is cut off from a certain form of communion with his fellow men, which pride, acting as a principle of destruction, tends to break down." (*The Philosophy of Existence*, p. 20.)

77—*The Philosophy of Existence*, p. 23.

78—*Ibid.*, p. 23.

79—*Ibid.*, p. 23.

80—*Ibid.*, p. 20.

81—*Ibid.*, p. 10.

82—*Ibid.*, p. 24.

83—Marcel speaks of a "reality's revelation of itself to us." He says, "to discover an intelligible relation, for example some mathematical relation whose eternal validity one suddenly recognizes ... is ... to have a sudden access to some reality's revelation of itself to us." (*The Mystery of Being*, vol. I, p. 53.)

84—*The Philosophy of Existence*, p. 95.

85—*Ibid.*, p. 95.

86—Marcel does not interpret experience as a condition to know a reality other than experience. He declares "beyond all experience, there is nothing; I do not say merely nothing that can be thought, but nothing that can be felt." (*The Mystery of Being*, vol. I, p. 48.)

87—*The Philosophy of Existence*, p. 8.

88—"This process of getting an insight has essentially nothing to do with the objective as such; we do not get an insight into something whose reality, by definition, lies completely outside our own." (*The Mystery of Being*, vol. I, p. 216.)

89—Marcel says, "The conviction that reality cannot be 'summed up,' that this is indeed the last way in which it can be apprehended, came to me very early, partly as a result of reading Bradley." (*The Philosophy of Existence*, p. 93.)

90—*Ibid.*, p. 8.

91—*Ibid.*, p. 8.

92—His emphasis is that "the more my existence takes on the character of including others, the narrower becomes the gap which separates it from being; the more, in other words, I am. This amounts to saying that there is no way in which we can conceive of being as something cut off from existence." (*The Mystery of Being*, vol. II, p. 33.)

93—Emmanuel Mounier points out in his *Existentialist Philosophies* that for Existentialism "the fundamental problem of philosophy is not so much existence in its widest sense as the existence of man." (p. 2, Rockliff, London, 1951.)

94—*The Philosophy of Existence,* p. 71.

95—*Ibid.,* p. 72.

96—*Ibid.,* p. 70.

97—*Ibid.,* p. 94.

98—*Ibid.,* p. 69.

99—*Ibid.,* p. 94.

100—*Ibid.,* p. 70.

101—*Ibid.,* p. 69.

102—In the Translator's Preface to Mounier's *Existentialist Philosophies* there is the interesting comment: "I am not at all sure what exactly is meant in this book by terms such as 'transcendence'." (p.v.) But Marcel is very explicit in some statements: "transcendence . . . is grasped through intimate lived experience—experience . . . intimately lived in the inner awareness of the poet or the artist." (*The Mystery of Being,* vol. I, p. 45.)

103—He declares, "I am not thinking of a norm in an abstract sense, some formal rule of ethics whose basis would be hard to discover and which would subsist somehow or other beyond the world of everyday experience, but rather to a certain fullness of life." (*Op. cit.,* vol. I, p. 202.) "In the manner of the Kantian philosophy," says Marcel, "one speaks of what lies outside, what lies beyond the limits of, experience. That, in the last analysis, can mean nothing, since the judging of something to be *outside* experience is itself empirical, that is to say it is a judgment made *from within* experience." (*Ibid.,* p. 46.) Whereas Marcel is interested exclusively in the judgment: Kant is not. Kant, therefore distinguishes *judgment about* a reality other than experience from such a reality, of whose properties, according to Kant, we know nothing, since we know only the organizing forms in our experience, and these are transcendental, or *a priori.*

104—*The Philosophy of Existence,* p. 22.

105—Marcel speaks of an individual relating himself to the "supra-human." "It transcends itself, or it tends to transcend itself, when it opens itself out to the experience of the supra-human." (*Philosophy of Existence,* p. 64-65.) But for him, the supra-human means "an experience which can hardly be ours in a genuine, and lasting way this side of death." One cannot emphasize too strongly that Marcel is preoccupied with the individual and the individual's experience, even though this should include more than this present life. Marcel does declare that "the most legitimate use it can make of its freedom is precisely to recognize that it does not belong to itself; this recognition is the starting point of its activity and creativeness." (*Ibid.*, p. 28.) But the emphasis is upon the individual's "recognition." Nothing whatsoever is mentioned about the *warrant* for such a recognition on the basis of an interpretation of the nature of the self as conditioned by a reality to which he relates himself in his freedom. Marcel also speaks of a "particle of light" when he declares: "I am obliged to bear witness because I hold, as it were, a particle of light, and to keep it myself would be equivalent to extinguishing it." (*Ibid.*, p. 70.) But he never mentions a word about the *status* or the *nature* of this "light," and nothing about what constitutes its *suitability* or its *adequacy* as a directive for life; and nothing about the *warrant* for accepting one "particle of light" rather than another. He declares, rather, that "I do not mean a light that could be understood—a meaningless phrase—but a light which is at the root of all and every understanding." (*The Mystery of Being*, vol. II, p. 124.)

106—*The Mystery of Being*, vol. I, p. 217.

107—*The Philosophy of Decadentism: A Study of Existentialism*, p. 16, Blackwell, Oxford, 1948. (Macmillan, N. Y.)

108—*Ibid.*, p. 28.

109—*Ibid.*, p. 29.

110—"We shall have to make an effort," says Marcel, "to . . . show that what matters today is that man should rediscover the sense of the eternal." (*The Mystery of Being*, vol. II, p. 165.) This explicitly states the scope of moral responsibility, according to Marcel. It is to cultivate a quality of experience—"the sense of the eternal." But, it may be pointed out that if there is an eternal reality, a knowledge of which is essential for human life, then discovery of its nature is a fundamental moral obligation. It is a moral obligation in so far as an adequate enlightenment of life is impossible without a discovery of the nature of the *total* context in which one endeavors to live.

111—As head of the Information Service organized by the Red Cross, Marcel was profoundly moved by the tragic sorrow of each individual. He says, "every index card was to me a heart rending personal appeal." (*The Philosophy of Existence*, p. 90.) It is his intense concern with the individual as *an individual* which accounts for his emphasis, and which accounts also for the particular character of his philosophical premise. He points out that a philosophy such as Spinoza's never attracted him, and he says, "perhaps because it seemed to me to leave no room for the concrete fullness of personal life." (*Ibid.*, p. 87.)

112—*The Mystery of Being*, vol. I, p. 23.

REFERENCE IN CHAPTER IV

1—Marcel speaks of a "stifling impression of sadness." (*The Philosophy of Existence*, p. 3.)

2—*Ibid.*, p. 18.

3—*Ibid.*, p. 18, (italics mine.)

4—*Ibid.*, p. 18.

5—*Ibid.*, p. 19.

6—*Ibid.*, p. 15.

7—*Meditations*, I, 21. Open Court, LaSalle, 1948.

8—*Ibid.*, IV, 66.

9—*Ibid.*, I, 22.

10—*Op. cit.*, p. 6.

11—*Ibid.*, p. 22.

12—*Ibid.*, p. 28.

13—*Ibid.*, p. 28.

14—*Ibid.*, p. 5.

15—One of the many contributions of Aristotle to moral theory is his insistence upon the difference between intellectual and moral virtue. There are, he maintains, intellectual virtues, and moral virtues; and they are not merely instances of the same class. Intellectual virtue includes "philosophical wisdom, understanding, and practical wisdom.' Philosophical intelligence he characterizes as speculation upon issues which do not necessarily relate to practice. Understanding, in distinction to philosophical intelligence, is a discriminating awareness of objects in practice. Practical wisdom in distinction to understanding is effectiveness in behavior. The three uses of intelligence, however, have one fundamental character in common which differentiates them from moral virtue. They do not necessarily involve a concern in the worthiness of the end for which intelligence is used. Yet, when this concern becomes a factor n the use of intelligence, a specifically moral problem is considered Differences in the worthiness of ends of effort constitute differences in the moral worthiness of intelligence itself. But an evaluation of intelligence from a moral point of view implies that intelligence is evaluated by a criterion other than intelligence. It is this difference which Aristotle emphasized when he pointed out that "in speaking about a man's character we do not say that he is wise or has understanding but that he is good-tempered or temperate." (*E. N.* I, 1103 a, 5-10.)

16—*Problems of Ethics,* p. 12, Trans. D. Rynin, Prentice-Hall, N. Y., 1939.

17—*Ibid.,* p. 17.

18—*Ibid.,* p. 21.

19—*Ibid.,* p. 19.

20—*Lectures in Psychoanalytic Psychiatry,* p. 25, Alfred Knopf, N. Y., 1946.

21—Spinoza believes that an individual is morally responsible when he understands that everything follows "from the necessity of its nature" and "comes to pass in accordance with eternal laws and rules." He furthermore believes that an individual who clearly understands this will also "endeavour to do well." But these two beliefs seem to be inconsistent; yet, what saves them from inconsistency is the sense of "endeavour." Spinoza does not say that an individual can *change* himself by making an effort to do so. What he says is that the endeavor of an individual to understand is his *nature.* The semblance of moral responsibility in "endeavour to do well" is, therefore, only verbal: it seems as if an individual were *morally responsible* for the initiative to understand. This action, however, is human nature. Human nature *by definition* is reasonable.

When an individual recognizes that a given condition is what it must necessarily be, he does not attempt to alter it. Moral worthiness, consequently, is confined to the intellectual effort to understand that the *given* is unalterable, and *must be accepted as it is.* Says Spinoza, "the more this knowledge that things are necessary is applied to particular things . . . the greater is the power of the mind over the emotions." Emotion, for Spinoza, means a confusion in man's life which arises when he does not understand that *the given* must be accepted as it is. For example, if one were to be sad because some day he must die, he would react emotionally to the *nature* of human life, rather than understandingly. This particular example of the immorality of refusing to accept what is inevitable is defensible; since it is as irrational to be dejected at the inevitability of death as it is to spend one's life pitying infants because they "cannot speak, walk, or reason." Most individuals would agree that *such* pity is sentimentality, and for the reason which Spinoza offers: it is the *nature* of an infant to be helpless, and all an individual's protest against it, will not alter it. Spinoza, therefore, was on the right track when he insisted that it is irrational to desire to change what is inevitable or unavoidable. But after recognizing that there are limits which existence sets upon reasonable desire, a morally matured individual *accepts* them; and then does *what he can within the limits of what is actually possible*. It is this responsibility, however, which Spinoza does not explore, and not by virtue of his indifference to human welfare; but by virtue of his deterministic metaphysic. This deterministic metaphysic he inherited from the science of the Renaissance, and within its point of view, he endeavoured to develop a moral philosophy. Hence he concluded that an individual's moral responsibility is not to alter existence, but to reflect upon it; to contemplate it; and to acquiesce to its unalterability. The moral end, he therefore maintains, is a "blessedness (which) consists in acquiescence of spirit."

22—Intellectual ability is without *moral* significance except in terms of what it enables one to accomplish in practice. It is this difference between intelligence as aptitude, and intelligence as practice, which Aristotle had in mind when he said that "intellect itself moves nothing, but only the intellect which aims at an end." (*E. N.* VI, 2, 1139a, 35.) Intellectual aptitude in excess of what is sufficient to inform an individual's actions of the conditions he must take into account for the enrichment of life is morally irrelevant. It is for this reason that so much philosophy itself is morally irrelevant; and so much theology is no more significant in terms of the "abundant life" than is symbolic logic.

The Gospel statement, "Whosoever hears these sayings of mine and does them, I will liken him unto a wise man" implies the disparagement of an intelligence which is mere aptitude, but not ability to make a difference in practice. It is a common observation in the New Testament that individuals see, and yet do not do; that they have opportunities to help bring into being the abundant life, and yet do not. The disparagement of mere intelligence is implied, for example, in the accusation, "you have seen me, and yet do not believe."

23—"By choosing what is good or bad," says Aristotle, "we are men of a certain character." (*E. N.* III, 2, 1112a, 2.) But an individual without intellectual ability to control the means to fulfill a desired end cannot even be said to *choose the end*. The choice of an end of action presupposes intelligence enough to interpret the end in terms of the means by which it is to be attained. "Choice" connotes action which is deliberately directed to attain an end which is desired. Such action implies a selection of what is believed to be an appropriate means for securing a desired end. Intelligence enough to inform behavior, therefore, is presupposed in morally significant judgment. A moral judgment would not even be passed upon acting if there were such a deficiency of intelligence that actions could not have the benefit of informed direction. Thus when a "choice is praised for being related to the right object," enough intelligence, as Aristotle has said, is presupposed for the action to be "rightly related to it." (*Ibid.*, 1112a, 7.) An actual error in selecting the appropriate means does not exempt an individual from moral accountability: the very possibility that he might have avoided error were he to do what he has ability enough to do is the ground for holding him morally accountable.

24—Aristotle points out the difference of an intellectual judgment and a moral choice. A judgment expresses opinion, and opinion, as he observes, relates "to all kinds of things, no less to . . . impossible things than to things in our own power." (*Ibid.*, 1111b, 2, 30.) But even in common convention the distinction is made between intellectual deficiency which is morally significant and intellectual deficiency which is not morally significant. When there isn't intelligence sufficient to inform activity, activity is not judged on the basis of moral responsibility, but only on the basis of aptitude. An individual, for example, is committed to an institution for the feeble minded, not for reasons of moral deficiency, but for reasons of intellectual deficiency. When an individual is not intelligent enough to control his behavior, he is not morally deficient, but intellectually deficient. This difference of intellectual inaptitude and moral deficiency is acknowledged in all court practices.

25—Understanding an obligation is an intellectual achievement: it is not necessarily a moral achievement. It becomes a moral achievement only when understanding enables an individual to fulfill the understood obligation. Thus as Bergson says, "even if our intelligence is won over, we shall never see in it anything but an explanation" unless more than an explanation is desired. (*Two Sources of Morality and Religion*, p. 25.) Only when individuals desire and endeavor to achieve benefits about which they are intellectually clear does intelligence have moral significance. It is not only what is thought which makes a fundamental moral difference in life: but what is done about what is thought.

26—Aristotle recognized that "it is not the same people that are thought to make the best choices and to have the best opinions." (*Ibid.*, III, 1112a, 8.) Socrates also observed this discrepancy between intelligence and intelligently informed actions when he pointed out to Protagoras that moral attainment involves more than an academic training of the mind. When he said that "the Athenians are an understanding people" he implied that their practice, nevertheless, does not always give evidence of their intelligence. This same distinction is reflected in the creation myth in the *Protagoras* in which Plato declares that "man has the wisdom necessary to the support of life (but) political wisdom he has not; for that is in the keeping of Zeus." Just how far this myth may be pressed for an understanding of Plato's point of view about the impossibility of attaining an enlightened political order is certainly a matter of conjecture. But the mention of such a point of view shows that Plato, although capable of formulating a utopian scheme of social order, nevertheless was aware of the disparity between intelligence as ability and intelligent living as taking advantage of such ability. It is Plato's point of view most likely which is expressed in the Socratic critique of the rationalistic optimism of Protagoras that all moral virtues can be taught—as if morality were merely an intellectual matter, and training were simply a clarification of ideas. The issue in the dialogue, therefore, is not whether reflection is morally significant or not, but whether a morally responsible life can be attained as Protagoras believed.

27—*The Two Sources of Morality and Religion,* p. 71, trans. R. A. Audra and C. Brereton, Holt, N. Y., 1935.

28—*Ibid.,* p. 42.

29—Normative morality, as decisions enlightened by all that *ought to be taken into account,* presupposes a capacity to understand principles. Hence, the "generality which primarily belongs to conceptual thought alone," to use a phrase of the late Professor Whitehead (*Process and Reality,* p. 23,) is a condition for morality. But that such capacity can be used for nothing except to formulate principles is certainly a genuine possibility. And it is a common fact that the utmost of generality is often detached from acting. Yet, although there is this possibility for speculative capacity to go to seed in detachment from practice, the very possibility of practice sufficiently informed of all that ought to be taken into account, nevertheless, presupposes that practice can be informed by generalizations.

30—The very difficulty of moral achievement is introducing into particular behavior situations a generality which saves action from the handicaps of uninformed particularity. An individual who gives attention to nothing but particular situations is identical with an animal in his behavior. An individual, on the other hand, whose sole concern is in general principles, and not in the application of them, is what Kierkegaard has called "comical," (*Concluding Unscientific Postscript,* p. 42, trans. D. F. Swenson, W. Lowrie, Princeton University, 1944.), since an unwillingness to use a principle for directing one's life denies the moral significance of reflecting. It ignores what Kierkegaard terms the "infinite need of a decision." (*Ibid.*, p. 33.)

The stipulation which Plato makes for a guardian is, therefore, instructive in this regard. Plato maintains that "neither the uneducated, nor yet those who never make an end of their education will be able ministers of state." (*Republic* VII, 519.) The practical administration of a state consists in coping with particular situations, but when there is no moral concern for practice, practice cannot be reflectively enlightened. The result is that practice remains uninformed, because the moral responsibility to use one's intelligence to direct practice is ignored. It is this very disregard for practice which makes Plato disqualify men from guardianship, who, after prolonged training in philosophy, cared to do nothing but philosophize. They were disqualified "because they will not act at all." (*Ibid.*, 519.)

31—Interest in an immediate object, to the exclusion of concern for a less immediate, may jeopardize life itself. This dilemma, however, which is caused by the intensity of desire, man shares in common with the animal. Just as there are situations in which impulse determines behavior to the detriment of an animal's life, so there are situations in which human well-being is put into jeopardy by impulse as the exclusive determinant of preference. A basic principle of preference is that interest is more intense in what is near than in what is remote. This implies that an immediate end of action has a significance for animal behavior which a less immediate end does not have. Hence, it is only the most developed of intelligence which informs choice by referring it to a remotely distant goal of interest. The achievement of this capacity, however, to control preference not by a proximity of objects, but by their value, is one essential trait of moral maturity.

Impulse, however, need not always be disparaged. There are situations in which impulse is a suitable determinant of acting, and there are times when the intensity of impulse is an advantage. Hence, if all preferences were intense as well as appropriate, their intensity would contribute instead of a precarious zest to life, a trustworthy drive. But, it is the incapacity of impulse to be informed of real requirements which constitutes its handicap. Impulse is attention confined to the immediate. The intensity of an interest constricts the area of attention to the interest itself. In this constriction of the area of awareness, the object for which there is intense interest reinforces the interest, so that the

165

intensity of interest excludes other factors from conditioning awareness itself. As John Dewey has said, impulse is not an entity which "rushes us off our feet": We act impulsively when we are rushed off our feet because inattentive to anything other than the satisfaction of an intense desire.

Satisfaction from fulfilled desire thus becomes a sort of biological "closed shop" in which objects that have given rise to satisfactions are the only ones which are likely to provide subsequent satisfactions. An object which is congenial to interest satisfies interest; and in so doing, prejudices interest for the object itself. This reinforcement of interest by objects congenial to it is a biological phenomenon which man shares with animal life. The significance of this biological fact for moral philosophy is no new discovery. Aristotle was clearly aware of the handicap to moral achievement by virtue of the animal predisposition to prefer objects which have already satisfied desire. He observed that "the exercise of appetite increases its innate force," and then made the significant generalization that "if appetites are strong and violent they expel the power of calculation." (*E. N.* III, 12, 1119b, 10-15.)

But the inability to calculate is the very nature of impulse as behavior. Impulse is a type of acting in which desire is the exclusive determinant of acting. Yet, it is this incapacity to respect requirements which are in opposition to the most assertive inclination of the moment that Spinoza calls "human bondage." When "a man is a prey to his emotions," says Spinoza, "he is not his own master," and although seeing that which is better for him, "is compelled to follow that which is worse."

The possibility for morally responsible behavior, therefore, rests upon the capacity to make choices which are not merely impulsive. Morality, however, does not imply a life without impulse: it implies that when there are obligations which must be considered, factors other than impulse must condition acting. The difficulty to inform decision is never underestimated by Aristotle. He is perfectly aware that "there is in the soul something different from reason which opposes and thwarts it." But the possibility of morality, he acknowledges, presupposes a capacity to control this factor.

Moral faith presupposes that man can operate upon the resources of his life to attain ends which are not within the range of animal achievement. But this point of view makes sense only when it is assumed that the animal factor in life is alterable. Unless the native endowments of human life can be controlled in the light of acknowledged human responsibilities, there would be in human life an inescapable and unalterable duality. Although there is an animal element in human resources for living, its alterability is an essential condition of moral responsibility. An operation upon impulsive inclination for human benefit is the moral task with which an individual is confronted by virtue of his animal endowments. Moral obligations, however, are not defined for an individual exclusively in terms of his native, or unlearned, animal resources. The responsibility to achieve the maximum benefit for human life involves the imposition of specifically human obligations upon unlearned endowments. "Nature's part," says Aristotle, "does not depend on us" (*E. N.* X, 9, 1179b, 21), but what native endowments *can* contribute to human well-being *does* depend upon what man does. It is for this specific achievement that man is *morally* responsible.

32—*E. N.* III, 1114a, 5-10.

33—Spinoza acknowledged that one condition for changing an individual's moral norm is to change his own conduct. He declares that after considering "whether it would not be possible to arrive at the new principles . . . without changing the conduct and usual plan of my life," he concluded that "with this end in view I made many efforts, but in vain."

REFERENCES IN CHAPTER V

1—Professor R. B. Perry says that "interest has the effect, so far as the interest-judgment is true, of transforming the object of that judgment from a problematic into an existent object; while mere judgment unattended by interest, has not such effect. This is what is meant by the impotence of the purely intellectual act." (*General Theory of Value,* p. 347.) This is the doctrine stated by William James in *The Will to Believe.* James declares that "There are . . . cases where a fact cannot come at all unless a preliminary faith exists in its coming." (*Op. cit.,* p. 25, Longmans, N. Y., 1927.) This same doctrine is basic to John Dewey's argument in "The Logic of Judgment of Practice": "The object of a practical judgment is some change, some alteration brought about in the given, the nature of which change depends upon the judgment itself, and yet constitutes the subject matter of judgment." (*Journal of Philosophy,* vol. XII, p. 521.)

2—Professor W. E. Hocking maintains that "In such regions the will-to-believe is justified, because it is not will to make-believe, but a veritable will to create the truth in which we believe." (*The Meaning of God in Human Experience,* p. 140, Yale, New Haven, 1942.) In this sense, faith is the "resolve which sees the world *as it is capable of becoming.*" (*Ibid.,* p. 148.)

3—Aristotle maintains that "in the case of the bad man there is equally present that which depends on himself in his actions even if not in his end." (*Ibid.,* III, 1114b, 20.)

4—*Ethics,* p. 28, trans. J. R. McCallum, Blackwell, Oxford, 1935.

5—*Concluding Unscientific Postscript,* p. 35.

6—Dewey, J., *Human Nature and Conduct,* p. 193, Holt, N. Y., 1922, Random House edition.

7—*The Intelligible World,* p. 342, Allen and Unwin, (Macmillan, N. Y.,) 1929.

8—Some sort of duality has been emphasized by many thinkers who have reflected on the nature of human life. Socrates suggested that human nature is like "the composite creations of ancient mythology,

168

such as the Chimera or Scylla or Cerberus . . . in which two or more different natures are said to grow into one." (*Republic,* IX, 588.) Goethe declares: "Two souls, alas! are lodg'd within my breast, Which struggle there for undivided reign." (*Faust,* Part I.) The nature of such contradiction, however, has often been interpreted in a way to ignore its *moral* significance.

A conflict of mutually exclusive desires has no *unique* moral significance: animals experience such conflicts. What is of unique moral significance, however, is that an individual whose nature includes animal desires is, when morally responsible, also aware of obligations to control and direct such desires. Hence, what makes a conflict of desires *morally* significant is the collision of an animal desire with an awareness of an obligation. The Gospel injunction, for example, "Love your enemies and pray for those who persecute you" (*Matthew* 5, 44.) presupposes this contradiction between an animal determinant of acting, and an obligation which must be fulfilled if an individual is to be worthy of Christian discipleship. An impulse to retaliate is animal; and the principle of "an eye for an eye" is an animal pattern of living. Every animal which acts upon impulse as the exclusive determinant of its behavior fulfils to perfection the *lex talionis.* But no human being who has no authority for life other than animal impulse would ever fulfil the injunction given by Jesus. This very injunction presupposes that there is an authority by which man can live which is other than the unlearned inclinations of animal life. It is this difference in authorities for living, therefore, which constitutes the radical distinction between *all* of animal life and *some* human life.

Conscience is an awareness of a disparity between what one is inclined to do, and what he is aware that he ought to do. Hence conflict is inevitable so long as the authority which one *accepts* as the criterion worthy of his respect is not an uncontested determinant in his decisions. Yet, according to some points of view, this very disparity between what an individual acknowledges he ought to do, and what he actually does, is so *radical* that the authority itself is irrelevant in actual practice. Kant, for example, maintains that "the distance separating the good which we ought to effect in ourselves from the evil whence we advance is infinite, and the act itself, of conforming our course of life to the holiness of the law, is *impossible of execution in any given time.*" (*Religion Within the Limits of Reason Alone,* p. 60, trans. T. M. Greene and H. H. Hudson, Open Court, Chicago, 1934, italics mine.) As stated, this point of view denies the possibility of the type of morality interpreted in this essay. *To the extent* that a norm is unrealizable in life, to that extent it is not a true *moral* criterion. The Sermon on the Mount, for example, constitutes a criterion which is achievable. In any situation in which an individual fulfils one of the injunctions in the Sermon on the Mount, in *that* situation he fulfils a normative principle, or requirement. In every situation in which an individual forgives another who injures him, he conforms to *one* of the Gospel commandments. That any individual will always conform to all of the injunctions in the Sermon on the Mount is improbable. It is improbable just because there is an animal ingredient which will always remain a factor with which an individual must cope, and which will *likely* affirm itself as *one* element in his decisions. But if an individual does forgive another who injures him, and does pray for another who despitefully treats him, in *that* moment in his life he *does fulfil* one injunction of the Gospel. *In that moment at least,* he experiences the blessedness promised by Jesus.

The norm which an individual acknowledges as the criterion by which he proposes to judge his life, and by means of which he proposes to measure his moral worthiness, is morally significant only if it offers specific guidance. But specific moral guidance is *particular* help in *particular* situations. Thus, the only norm which is morally significant is the particularity of morally helpful instruction which constitutes the relevance of a *moral* norm to actual decision. The Beatitudes in the Sermon on the Mount, for example, are particular *moral* directives, or principles, just because they stipulate *specific* requirements.

"Thou shalt love thy neighbor as thyself" (*Matt.,* 19, 19.) is a norm which assumes that an individual comes into relations with others in *particular* situations in which there are occasions for anger and revenge. It implies that there are situations in which an individual in relation to another is involved in tension, friction, and conflict. What is also implied is that in these situations an authority other than impulse is likewise possible. The *moral* significance, therefore, of the injunctions given by Jesus is their relevance to *particular* situations in an individual's life. This presupposes their applicability to the circumstances which constitute the sources of strife. "If thou wilt enter into life, keep the commandments" (*Ibid.,* 19, 17.), affirms that in the many particular situations of life there are general requirements which must be respected if an individual is to do what Jesus stipulates he ought to do. Every time an individual enters into relation with another, conflict is potential. All of these particular situations can, however, be saved from conflict with its tragic injury to man's life, both of body and soul, by conforming to the Gospel authority for life: "If your brother injure you, instruct him; and if he repents for his offense, forgive him." (*Luke* 17, 3.)

Forgiving another who injures one is a general instruction because it is a principle applicable to *all* human relationships in which individuals offend each other. The general injunction, however, is applicable to all particular instances in which one is injured by another. The applicability of this moral directive is stressed by the insistence of Jesus that if one is offended many times, so many times must he also forgive. Every time one forgives another who injures him, so many times does he fulfil the commandment. And every time he introduces into his life the authority proposed by Jesus, so many times he saves himself and others from the tragic consequences of acting upon a less worthy authority.

When "an eye for an eye" is demanded, life comes under the animal authority of vindictive pugnacity. But when an individual conforms to the directives affirmed in the Sermon on the Mount, he transcends an animal determinant in life, while yet retaining animal endowments. Acknowledging the duality of possible determinants in acting, however, does not imply a *radical duality* in endowments in man's nature. A duality in determinants for acting is not a duality in the nature of an individual whose life itself ought to become unified in its allegiance to a morally worthy authority. The doctrine of a radical duality in endowments fails to acknowledge that even the animal ingredients in human life are capable of moral use. Yet, normative moral achievement rests upon the possibility of bringing animal endowments under a more than animal determinant.

Every individual who conforms to the Gospel injunction demonstrates what human life with animal endowments can be in situations in which animal determinants would otherwise be the exclusive authority. In trying situations, such individuals demonstrate the actual capacity of human life to conform to more than an animal authority, and to do what an animal authority does not require of life.

Dualism of some sort is implied in an acknowledgment of moral authority; but the kind of dualism which is implied is *the critical issue* in a moral philosophy. One type of dualism is essential to the nature of morality; whereas, another is the repudiation of its very possibility. An interpretation of moral dualism which maintains that the moral end is in *radical* opposition to the animal resources of human life repudiates the possibility of morality as here interpreted. It implies that the objective of moral life is radically other than its elemental endowments.

But this theory is basically false, since in every social relation *some* animal factor is involved. The moral tragedy in human relations is that the animal factors constitute the *only* determinants for decisions. For the individual whose action in a social situation is not exclusively determined by animal impulse, but by a moral authority, such as the Sermon on the Mount, there is no *radical* dichotomy of animal ingredients in human life and the moral end. The moral end is directing *all* of an individual's capacities for living by *a more-than-animal* authority for living. Such an authority, however, is applicable to human life with animal endowments just because human life has *more-than-animal capacities*. With animal endowments, man does not live in a *purely* animal context; and therefore he has more than merely animal requirements to fulfill. If man did not have these requirements imposed upon him by the moral end itself of living as he ought in his social relations, he would not be under the moral obligation to introduce into his life more than animal determinants.

A dualistic theory which maintains that an individual is divided into two irreconcilable components, such as is implied in the figures proposed by Socrates and Goethe, implies that an individual with animal endowments *cannot* be unified into a functioning system of interests on a level which is more than animal. The very possibility of moral achievement, however, is operating upon animal resources by *a more-than-animal* authority. The moral desirability of this imposition of *a more-than-animal* authority upon life is that an individual with animal endowments has more than merely animal capacities for living. The Sermon on the Mount is morally significant just because it declares what life may be that animal life is not.

It is, of course, intelligible to speak of the "higher" and "lower" self, as Abailard does (*Ethics,* p. 18), or of the "better self" and "a worse self," as Bradley does (*Ethical Studies,* p. 276), but such duality must not be constructed to be a radical opposition in natures making up an individual. If there were two radically different natures making up an individual, a moral unification or integration would be impossible. The possibility of moral unification, however, presupposes that the materials with which the moral process of integration must operate are amenable to such integration. If there were two natures constitutive of an individual, as distinct as the Zoroastrian principles of Darkness and Light, or as irreconcilable as the Pythagorean principles of Good and Bad, unification would simply be impossible. The moral end, however, is a unified life: it is a life integrated by an allegiance to a morally worthy authority which directs with consistency the diverse ingredients in an individual's life.

"An eye for an eye" is one principle for living. "Pray for those who persecute you" (Matthew, 5, 44.) is another principle for living. Both of these principles are potential authorities for human life. But they are as radically opposed as any of the dualistic opposites of the Pythagoreans, the Zoroastrians, or the Manichaeans. Yet, irreconcilable as they are, both *may* become the exclusive determinant of any individual's life. From the duality of potential authorities for life, however, nothing may be inferred about an irreconcilable duality *within human nature*. It is the metaphorical limitations of language which account for the pictorial concepts of a radical dualism of natures constitutive of human nature.

Ascetic theory takes such presumed dualism at full face value, and makes no provision for pictorial metaphors. Asceticism is a serious effort to cope with the moral problem as it is implied in a theory of a radical dualism of natures. An ascetic seeks the moral end by denying as many of the animal requirements of human life as he possibly can. But he obviously cannot deny all of them. He must have food; and he must sleep; just as any animal must. The moral problem, consequently, is not to repudiate all animal requirements in life; but rather to direct them.

The material with which the moral task is undertaken is not itself a moral "evil:" it is its use without adequate direction which becomes a moral evil. One source of moral evil is a consequence of expressing animal impulses with insufficient instruction of the human requirement. Moral evil is thus derivative: it is secondary to a wrong use of resources for living. But such default is morally significant because it is avoidable. What is unavoidable is that there are animal ingredients in human life: what is avoidable is their expression merely as animal reactions without morally informed use.

An individual who is aware that one use is more desirable than another is aware of moral distinctions within experience. This is a duality *within experience* in the sense that one quality of life is acknowledged as more desirable than another. But this distinction between different ways of living is not a radical opposition within the nature of an individual. What is radically opposed are the types of living; and although both are potential patterns for an individual, both are exclusive of each other in consistent acting.

A morally serious individual is aware of a disparity between what he desires, and what he acknowledges he ought to desire. But this difference is not a fundamental opposition within his nature: the opposition is within the uses of his capacities for living. One use constitutes one quality of living: another use constitutes another quality of living. The decision to use resources in ways which will contribute to a morally worthy quality of life is a moral decision. Moral sensitivity is the awareness that there is more to be achieved in character than one has already achieved; and it is this sensitivity to the disparity between one's authority for life and his actual life which is moral conscience. It is, therefore, unthinkable that a morally serious individual should ever come to the point of view that he has done all that it is conceivable should be done; and that he has transcended the disparity itself between what he is, and what he acknowledges he ought to be.

An animal impulse which is an expression of physiological function is neither moral nor immoral. What is moral is the way it is expressed: it is the effectiveness with which it is incorporated into a system of human requirements. What is immoral is likewise the way it is expressed. Hunger, for example, is an impulse which can, and must, be assimilated into a system of human requirements. But the pugnacity with which some animals defend themselves against every provocation cannot be incorporated into a pattern of human life without jeopardizing, or completely destroying, social order. It is such an elemental impulse which J. S. Mill had in mind when he said that there are "bad instincts"; and in so far as man has such animal factors in his life, he has the urgent moral responsibility to avert their tragic social consequences.

The pattern of life recommended by Jesus is one specific way to cope with such animal factors. When accused by Pilate, "he gave no answer, not even to a single charge." (*Matt.*, 27, 14.) The reason Pilate "wondered greatly" is obvious: he saw demonstrated before his eyes one way that anger can be controlled.

Giving up one way of living is a condition for attaining another. This is a fundamental principle of all life. Everything which is chosen implies a rejection of whatever is incompatible with it. Hence the nature of moral unification presupposes that elements which are contradictory of each other must be altered. The effectiveness, however, of methods for altering such factors gives rise to many disputes among philosophers and psychologists, and the contribution of modern psychoanalysis is rich in pointing out the moral peril of some methods for coping with unacceptable impulses.

The possibility, nevertheless, for a moral unification of life rests upon the adaptability of animal ingredients to uses which are not animal. If the animal ingredients in man's life could not be adapted to other than animal uses, an acknowledgment of specifically human obligations would constitute an insoluble disunity in human life. An elementary fact of animal behavior, however, is that instinctive capacities *can* be taught new functions. There is no end of evidence of this fact in the training of animals to do what they otherwise would never have done without such learned discipline. A dog, for example, which is trained to lead a blind person is taught a behavior pattern which has no counterpart in purely animal activity. Thus, in the training of an animal for an other-than-instinctive function, an animal demonstrates the adaptability of animal endowments to acquired uses.

The presupposition of adaptability of man's native endowments to social requirements is so fundamental in the thought of Plato that his whole philosophy of education rests on it. Education, according to Plato, is an operation upon an unlearned endowment in order to direct it into uses which are contributory to well-being for the individual as well as for the group. Education, for Plato, is a basis for radically different patterns of living. The *elemental* basis for all human life is the same: the moral differences in human life arise from the direction given to this elemental basis. The direction of an animal ingredient into a pattern of life which provides well-being for the individual in his group, and for the group through the contribution of the individual, is, for Plato, the nature of education. (*Republic* III, 410; VI, 495; VII, 519.) The direction which is given through discipline to the unlearned resources native to human life is a moral operation upon non-moral elements; and the direction of the resources of life to moral ends is the radical moral differentiation of individuals. But radical as the moral distinctions may be, there is an elemental basis which men have in common, and which constitutes *the given* which they use so differently.

It is, therefore, false theory to maintain that the unlearned animal factors in human life, as such, constitute moral "goods;" and that instinctive drives are moral ends. Instinctive impulses may be used for moral ends when they are used in ways contributory to human well-being; otherwise they have no more moral significance in man than they have in the animal. It is the use to which any resource for life is put which determines its moral value. All sound moral distinctions, therefore, are based on an estimate of the suitability of a particular *use* in light of particular requirements which an individual is under obligation to respect. A failure to do what one acknowledges he ought to do is a disparity between what is accomplished, and what an individual is aware might have been accomplished. What makes such a deficiency morally significant is that it is a consequence of an individual's failure to do what he ought to have done to prevent it. The deficiency is not merely the absence of something: what ought to have been done has been positively neglected. Such neglect is an action: it is an individual's decision to do less than he acknowledges he ought to do.

An individual's awareness of the difference between what he is, and what he acknowledges he ought to be, is a moral distinction. The distinction between achievement, and the norm by which an individual approves his achievement, is a moral judgment. Hence moral judgment is an evaluation of life by reference to a criterion of worthiness. When the criterion to which an individual refers his life is regarded as a divine reality, the judgment upon his life is not only moral; but also religious. The distinction between a moral judgment, and a religious judgment is thus a difference in the nature of the criteria by which life is evaluated. An individual who proposes to judge his life by a divine norm is religious. But the act of judging his life by such a criterion is moral. The essential difference, therefore, between a religious individual who is morally serious, and a non-religious individual who is also morally serious, is a difference in the criteria each acknowledges as the norms by which the worthiness of life is to be measured.

9—*E. N.*, II, 1105b, 15.
10—*Ibid.*, III, 1112a, 1-5.
11—*Op. cit.*, p. 46.
12—*Ibid.*, p. 32.
13—*Ibid.*, p. 44.
14—*Phaedrus*, 274. Trans. B. Jowett, Oxford, 1931.
15—*Op. cit.*, X, 1178a, 35.
16—*Op. cit.*, p. 121.
17—*Ibid.*, X, 1178b, 2.
18—*Republic* X, 617.
19—*Op. cit.*, II, 1104a, 30-35.
20—A mechanistic determinist, just as a fatalist, argues that whatever one does is what he could not avoid doing. But what an individual does does not necessarily indicate what he might have done. Although the dogma of fatalism, like the dogma of mechanistic determinism, cannot be refuted; yet, if it is accepted, moral responsibility cannot be maintained. The doctrine that everything is already determined implies that decision is not an individual's responsibility. Moral earnestness, which is a resolve to make a beneficial difference in the significance

176

of human life, would, therefore, be discredited by a belief that reality cannot be changed, and that whatever is, is what it will be, notwithstanding what an individual does.

21—Bernard Bosanquet says that "the really typical choices—those which show human freedom and the true nature of initiative in their fullest, are the great logical choices which occupy years in the making, as when a man chooses his religion, or his profession . . . working . . . til he has found, or nearly found, a self-expression which includes the whole of him." (*Science and Philosophy*, "The Prediction of Human Conduct," p. 233, Macmillan, N. Y., 1927.)

22—The moral significance of a decision implies a sense of urgency. The confrontation of an individual by an acknowledged obligation implies that time-limits for acting are defined in the obligation itself. What must be done promptly if it is to be done at all stipulates a time-interval for acting. When there is just so much time to do something which will make a difference to human well-being, the limitation of time defines the limitation of the possibilities for coping with the situation. It is for this reason that Kierkegaard declares that "the time itself is the task." (*Op. cit.*, p. 147.) The moral challenge of a particular situation is that a morally matured individual acknowledges that he is confronted by a responsibility: his responsibility is to do all he can do with his resources in time to make the beneficial difference which he himself acknowledges is his opportunity, and so, his obligation.

The decisiveness of a situation in which an individual's action makes a difference is the moral interpretation of time. Time has meant many different things for speculative philosophy; but it means one very specific thing for moral earnestness. It means that when a matter of import for human life is at stake, an individual must accept his responsibility to do what he can for the benefit of human life. No matter how naive such a morally earnest sense of time may be, it is clear that there is no comparable sense of moral urgency in the Kantian doctrine of time. When time is a form of perception, as it is with Kant, an individual is not confronted by the urgency to make a particular decision lest it be too late to do so later. The moral significance of time interpreted as decisive events in which issues are resolved one way or another is presupposed by moral earnestness. Kierkegaard's condemnation of speculative philosophy, for example, which treats moral issues as concepts, and not as challenges for decision, can be explained only by the moral earnestness with which he regarded time. Brunner points out that "Existential thinking means thinking in a way which involves one's whole life. It

177

means the attitude of one who is at every moment involved in the question at issue, that is, of one who is no mere spectator. 'Existentiality' is the very opposite of all that is academic, abstract, or theoretical. We think 'existentially' when we are conscious that for us matters of life and death are at stake." Kierkegaard's rejection of Hegelian philosophy rests ultimately upon the nature of time, for as Brunner has pointed out, Hegel "transformed time into a concept," and by so doing, removed from human life its moral seriousness." (*The Mediator,* p. 382, Westminster, Philadelphia, 1947, Trans. Olive Wyon.)

23—*E. N.* I, 1096b, 30-35.
24—*Ibid.,* VII, 1153b, 15.
25—*Ibid.,* I, 1099b, 5.
26—*Ibid.,* I, 1099b, 5.
27—*Ibid.,* I, 1099b, 5ff.
28—*Ibid.,* IX, 1170b, 15.
29—*Meditations,* VII, 68.
30—*Ibid.,* VI, 50.
31—*Ibid.,* XI, 18.
32—Fichte has inaccurately stated the Stoic's position in Lecture IV of *The Way Towards the Blessed Life* when he says that "there is but one thing needful to him—not to despise himself; beyond this he wills nothing, needs nothing, and can use nothing." What the Stoic maintains, rather, is that when he has done what he acknowledges he ought to do, he will not despise himself. Saving himself from despising himself is not, however, the moral end for which he proposes to live. When he achieves a control over his reactions to the adversities of nature and the cruelties of men, he does not censor himself. But what it is desirable to avoid is not what he regards as the one desirable end in life.
33—*Op. cit.,* I, 1097b, 1.
34—*Ibid.,* X, 1176b, 30.
35—*Philebus,* 60.
36—*Op. cit.,* IX, 1169b, 28.
37—*Ibid.,* I, 1098b, 15-20.
38—*Ibid.,* IX, 1169b, 30.
39—The most elementary of moral reflection is aware of this disparity between particular desires and the system of the self in which they arise. An attainment of a morally worthy well-being would constitute no problem if it were synonymous with satisfactions of particular desires. Moral philosophy would, consequently, never have developed had the moral problem been no more profound than the striving to find means to fulfill the most assertive of desires.
40—*Phaedrus,* 256.

41—*Op. cit.*, IX, 1166b, 25.

42—A religious individual refers to a divine reality as the criterion by which he assesses the worthiness of his decisions. But his interpretation of the obligations which are imposed upon his life by a divine reality is conditioned by his moral development. Hence the difference between a religious and a non-religious individual is not necessarily a moral difference. It is rather a difference in the interpretation of the nature of the norm by which they assess their lives. A morally earnest individual may, in fact, impose upon himself a norm more rigorous in moral demands than a religious individual; but a religious individual believes that the norm to which he ought to conform is a reality which is not a product of his own, or another's morally earnest efforts.

The moral norm formulated by Kant, for example, is not a religious criterion, because Kant does not maintain that the imperative imposed upon reasonable life is external to reasonable life itself. The Categorical Imperative is a requirement which reason imposes upon life for its reasonable direction. Kant does not maintain that the normative authority for human life is a divine imperative: it is rather an imperative which man formulates for himself. A religious individual believes that there is a divine reality which is the authority by which he ought to live. His primary concern, therefore, is the conformity of his life to its stipulations; and the earnestness with which one endeavours to fulfill the requirements he believes are imposed upon him by a divine reality is authentic religion.

The mere belief that there is a divine reality, however, does not constitute religious faith. A belief that there is a divine reality is religious faith only when the belief makes a difference in man's life, because it confronts him with a moral responsibility. It is the actual effort to do what he believes he is responsible for which indicates that he *really* believes that there are requirements which are mandatory. An individual who acknowledges a divine reality, but who ignores its authority in his life, declares by his own way of living that the divine reality is morally irrelevant in his life. A religious individual believes that there is a supranatural reality, and *purely* speculative systems of philosophy also rest upon a belief that there is a supranatural reality. Parmenides, for example, formulated a philosophy on the basis of a premise that there is an eternal One which is other than the changing world. Yet, this One is not religiously significant for Parmenides since it does not confront him with *specific* responsibilities in his life. The religious significance of a reality for an individual is expressed by what an individual does to take it into account in his life. A dualism, therefore,

179

is implied in a religious interpretation of a divine authority for life, just as a dualism is implied in every interpretation of a moral authority, even though it is not a divine reality transcendent of man's life.

The Imperative which Kant formulates as a mandatory requirement for a reasonable individual is as mandatory for an individual who desires to live reasonably as are the divine commandments for a religious individual who desires to live in conformity to such requirements. The earnestness of a religious individual to fulfill the requirements imposed upon his life by virtue of his relation to a divine reality may not differ from the zeal of an equally earnest individual to conform to an imperative he formulates for the direction of his life. What differentiates a religiously earnest individual and a morally earnest non-religious individual is the *status of the authorities* to which each endeavors to conform. The authority by which a religious individual proposes to live is a reality whose *existence* is believed to be independent of human life. The authority, on the other hand, by which a non-religious, yet morally earnest individual proposes to live is acknowledged to be a product of human life.

Kant, for purely philosophical reasons, does not give a religious interpretation to the Categorical Imperative. He maintains that man can know no reality external to the content of his own experience, or transcendent of his own *a priori* endowments. This implies that whatever can be known is confined to human resources. Kant could not, therefore, construe the ultimate moral authority for life in religious terminology. He could not, for example, say that the ultimate authority for life is the Will of God. It is, therefore, indefensible to say that Kant maintains that moral evil is "the self-determination of the will in opposition to the Law of God." For purely philosophical reasons, Kant could not say this. What he did maintain, however, is that "evil is the positive resistance of the will to the law of good." But for Kant, the law of good, and the Law of God should not be identified. That they may be identified, Kant could not deny on the basis of his philosophical premises. That they are not identifiable, he likewise could not affirm, and yet be consistent with his philosophical premises. According to his presuppositions, the content of knowledge is *confined* to human experience, and hence there is no warrant to claim knowledge of any reality transcendent of experience.

Religious faith, however, includes the conviction than man *can* attain a knowledge of a reality transcendent of human life, and *can* therefore direct his life by a reality which does not have its origin in the very life itself which is in need of trustworthy direction. Religious faith is that an individual's most dependable help does not have its source within human resources, but transcend*ent* of them. It is in reference to such a reality that Saint Augustine passes moral judgment upon himself. He does not find himself deficient by standards which he assumes he *projects;* but which he believes *confront* him by virtue of their existence transcend*ent* of his life: "To God being perfect, is (man's) imperfection displeasing."

The disparity between what an individual is inclined to do, and what he believes he ought to do which is worthy of his relation to a divine reality, constitutes a dualism in every genuinely earnest religious life. Yet, if an individual were convinced that no completely trustworthy direction could be given to his life apart from his relation to a divine reality, he would not make a radical dichotomy of religious and moral means for attaining the good life. He would rather maintain that man's religious faith makes an *indispensable* contribution to human well-being by providing human life with a clue for the progressive discovery of a completely trustworthy authority for living. If man were incapable of knowing such a divine reality, it would run counter to all moral sensitivity that he should hold himself responsible for his failure to know it. Although the disparity between what man is, and what he believes he ought to be by virtue of his relation to the divine reality, is never denied by an earnest religious individual, this disparity, nevertheless, is acknowledged by a morally earnest religious individual as his failure to do what he is able to do.

An insistence upon the complete helplessness of man repudiates the moral significance of religious faith itself. The doctrine of the Divine Initiative as the *one and only* condition for the attainment of human blessedness implies that man is not even morally responsible for his own failure to orient his life to the Divine Reality. But every time in the history of theological doctrine that this notion has arisen as a way to attribute gratitude to God for whatever good man attains in his life the result *in doctrine* has been the moral irrelevance of man's decisions, and the moral meaninglessness of human responsibility. A human life is morally serious only when it acknowledges that it is responsible for its decisions; and any theological doctrine which discredits this basic moral faith thereby repudiates moral faith. But an individual who seriously assumes his responsibility to improve either the quality of his own life, or to help another beneficially alter the character of his life, believes that something can be done which is worthy of him to do. This faith presupposes, however, that an individual is capable of directing himself by one or another authorities for living. A fundamental difference in the moral significance of authorities is a duality in authorities.

The history of religion, as Otto points out, is a "gradual shaping and filling in (of religious faith) with ethical meaning." (*The Idea of the Holy*, p. 6, Oxford, London, 1943, Trans. J. W. Harvey.) Yet, the most elementary religious faith is not "ethically neutral." If it were, the historical association of moral earnestness with religious faith would be incidental to religious faith itself. But the very acknowledgment of man's dependence upon an ultimate reality transcendent of his life is a morally significant religious faith. Man's interpretation of its nature, however, is morally conditioned, since his interpretation, or understanding of its nature, cannot be morally more matured than he himself is. A religious belief, for example, which is affirmed in the Bhagavad-Gita is that "he cometh unto me whose works are done for me; who esteemeth me supreme; who is my servant only . . . who liveth amongst all men without hatred." (*Eleventh Discourse,* quoted from *The Nature of Religion,* Georg Wobbermin, p. 201, Crowell, N. Y., 1933.) According to this religious belief, *living without hatred among men,* is an absolute moral requirement. It is also a specifically *religious* obligation because it is believed to be a condition for man's worthiness to enter into relationship with the divine reality. Man's interpretation, however, of the nature of this reality conditions what he believes is worthy of his relationship to it; and it is only when the divine reality is believed to be concerned with the welfare of *all* men that an individual finds in his assumed relationship to it a responsibility imposed upon him to be mindful of and concerned with the welfare of *all* men. Yet, only a morally sensitive individual could be aware of an ethical responsibility in his relationship to what he regards the ultimate reality which confronts him with responsibilities to others. The religious faith of Saint Augustine, for example, is that God "so carest for every one of us, as if (he) carest for him only; and so for all, as if they were but one." (*Confessions,* III.) This faith manifestly presupposes a moral development which is not common to all individuals who believe they are ultimately dependent upon a divine reality for their welfare. Although it is a universal religious conviction that there is a *completely dependable reality* to which man may turn for help in his life, the specific significance which man discovers in this reality is not universal. It is conditioned by what man has done to prepare himself to understand its full significance for his life. Man's capacity to interpret the moral significance of the divine reality is, therefore, a limit which moral conditioning itself places upon the moral benefit of religious faith.

43—*On the Trinity,* III, iii, 8; Clark, Edinburgh, 1873.
44—*Confessions,* VII.

INDEX

Abailard, 126, 127, 128, 129
abstraction, 12, 13, 20, 74, 82, 85, 133, 146
acceptability, social, 7
accountability, moral, 22
activisim, 87
activity, 87, 88
  animal, 22
  purposive, 109
  reflective, 13
  selective, 22
actualism, ethical, 3
adaptability, 174, 175
adequacy, 42, 52
alterability, 165 n.31
analysis, phenomenological, 74
anarchy, 88
anthropology, 9
anti-authoritarian, 3
anti-social, 27
approval, 34, 104, 137
Aristotle, 10, 12, 19, 20, 21, 22, 23, 24, 25, 26, 31, 47, 74, 115, 121, 126, 127, 135, 138, 139, 140, 141, 143, 146, 148, 160 n.15, 162 n.22, 163 n.26
assent, 125
assumption, 34, 42, 57, 66, 141
assurance, 141
attainability, 138
Augustine, St., 59, 149, 181, 182
Aurelius, M., 142
authority, 5, 19, 48, 62, 64, 65, 97, 114, 119, 124, 126, 146, 171, 172, 179 n.42
  divine, 180

behavior, 12, 21, 22, 137, 165 n.31
Behaviorism, 134
belief, 32
  Christian, 63
benefit, 121, 127, 129, 130, 131, 132, 177 n.22
Bergson, H., 111, 163 n.25
Bhagavad-Gita, 181
Bobbio, N., 87, 93, 94
Bosanquet, B., 28, 177 n.21
Bradley, F. H., 172
bribery, 27
Brill, A. A., 107
Brunner, E., 17 n.22

causation, 34, 135

challenge, 39, 138, 177 n.22
character, 26, 115, 131, 134, 135, 136, 160 n.15
choice, 1, 28, 137, 148, 162 n.23, 177 n.21
Church, Christian, 30, 85
commandment, 2, 62, 92, 93, 170, 171
Commandments, Ten, 18, 95
commitment, 122, 125, 134
community, 130
conditions, moral, 138, 139, 141, 148
conformity, 10, 21
conscience, 166 n.8, 174
consistency, 41
contradiction, 26, 27, 53, 81, 168 n.8
control, 27, 42, 143, 178 n.32
convention, 15, 16, 17, 19, 49, 50, 51, 54, 62
conviction, 18, 31, 32, 67, 98, 108, 125, 181, 182
courage, 35, 36, 37
criterion, formal, 23, 170
  moral, 1, 7, 9, 20, 22, 23, 25, 32, 33, 34, 39, 42, 87, 103, 117, 129, 133, 160 n.15, 176, 179 n.42
  religious 179 n.42
custom, 6, 7, 8, 49, 50, 51
Cynic, 53, 54
Cynicism, 48, 52, 103

deception, 29
decision, 2, 3, 4, 29, 60, 67, 110, 121, 148, 174, 176, 177 n.22, 179 n.42, 181
deficiency, 23
definition, 35, 36, 143
Democritus, 46, 47, 48, 49, 50, 51, 52, 53, 54
Demos, R., 19
Descartes, R., 93
desirability, 102, 130, 138, 144
desire, 26, 102, 124, 129, 130, 144, 147, 148, 149
despair, 89
determinants, 122, 141, 171, 172
determinism, metaphysical, 115, 136, 137, 161 n.21, 176 n.20
Dewey, J., 165 n.31, 168 n.1
direction, 2, 120, 132, 162 n.23, 179 n.42, 180, 181
directive, 1, 2, 3, 5, 11, 12, 16, 22, 66, 95, 97, 113, 118, 159 n.105

claims, 37, 38, 49, 67
  theory of, 37, 45, 46, 48, 49, 53, 54,
    56, 57, 58, 61, 66, 67, 70, 86

language, 47, 48, 50, 65, 173
laws, 68, 83, 96, 168 n.8
Locke, J., 119
logic, 14
loyalty, 51, 86

Marcel, G., 71-88
mean, 23, 24, 25
metaphysic, 4, 7, 48, 49, 50, 51, 74, 76
Mill, J. S., 103, 174
morality, 7, 20, 21, 23, 27
  conventional, 24, 25
mores, 2, 6, 8
motivation, 11, 121
motive, 8, 16, 38, 56, 128

nihilism, 48
norm, 8, 9, 3, 24, 37, 38, 39, 41, 45, 103,
  104, 115, 148, 170, 176, 179 n.42

obligation, moral, 23, 36, 39, 45, 100,
  110, 114, 118, 124, 127, 145, 159 n.110,
  165 n.31, 177 n.22, 182
ontology, 80
order, 15, 19
  corporate, 5
Orphic, 94
Otto, R., 182
ought, 27, 28, 29, 38, 39, 43, 122, 126,
  144, 146, 148, 176, 179 n.42, 181

Parmenides, 179 n.42
pattern, ordering, 15, 16, 48
Perry, R. B., 28, 151 n.41, 168 n.1
pessimism, 48
Philebus, 144
philosopher, moral, 14, 16, 22, 38
philosophy, existentialist, 55
  moral, 8, 9, 11, 12, 13, 15, 16, 17, 19,
    20, 21, 22, 24, 25, 26, 27, 31, 32, 34,
    39, 43, 44, 45, 46, 52, 55, 61, 95, 103,
    106, 108, 144, 178 n.39
Pius XII, Pope, 2, 3
Plato, 14, 15, 16, 17, 18, 19, 20, 21, 31,
  55, 57, 129, 135, 147, 148, 164 n.30
pleasure, 144, 145, 146, 148
practice, 12, 13, 17, 22, 118, 164 n.29
  conventional, 17, 25, 26, 34
  particular, 16, 21
pragmatism, 4, 17

predictability, 136
preference, 85, 121, 122, 123, 143, 165
  n.31
prejudice, 29
premise, 41, 42, 44, 47, 48, 53, 54, 72, 94,
  108, 159 n.111, 179 n.42, 180
presupposition, 22, 33, 69, 71, 72, 124,
  136, 137, 175, 180
pride, 28, 29, 79, 91
principle, basic, 22, 24, 25
  metaphysical, 49
  moral, 1, 2, 4, 5, 10, 11, 12, 13, 14, 15,
    16, 17, 18, 20, 22, 38, 40, 42, 43, 50,
    55, 71, 85, 95, 113, 125, 164 n.30,
    170
  ordering, 19, 38
  universal, 19
problem, moral, 2, 14, 15, 23, 31, 34, 36,
  37, 38, 39, 77, 88, 100, 147, 149, 160
  n.15, 173, 178 n.39
  philosophical, 35, 40, 87, 88, 118
progress, moral, 112
proposition, 36, 37, 143
Protagoras, 45, 46, 152 n.9, 163 n.26
psychiatry, 107
psychoanalysis, 174
psychology, 74, 75
Pythagorean, 23, 172, 173

quest, 32, 37

rationalism, philosophical, 26, 28, 29,
  151 n.42
reality, divine, 179 n.42, 180, 181, 182,
  183
  theory of, 46, 48, 53
reasoning, 151 n.42
reflection, 26, 31, 126
  moral, 10, 12, 14, 21, 25, 133, 178 n.39
regret, 133
repentance, 148
requirements, 3, 92, 149, 165 n.31, 173,
  175, 179 n.42, 182
responsibility, 22, 23, 29, 30, 63, 96, 99,
  100, 101, 102, 105, 106, 108, 109, 114,
  115, 126, 128, 132, 134, 135, 136, 161
  n.21, 179 n.42, 181
Royce, J., 27, 151 n.38
rule, 13, 14, 21, 23, 24, 25

sacrifice, 24, 25, 127
satisfaction, 147, 165 n.31, 178 n.39
Schlick, M., 104, 105, 106
Schweitzer, A., 22, 111